Censorship

ISSUES
(previously Issues for the Nineties)

Volume 27

Editor

Craig Donnellan

Independence
Educational Publishers

First published by Independence
PO Box 295
Cambridge CB1 3XP
England

British Library Cataloguing in Publication Data
Censorship – (Issues Series)
I. Donnellan, Craig II. Series
363.3'1

ISBN 1 86168 056 2

Printed in Great Britain
City Print Ltd
Milton Keynes

Typeset by
Claire Boyd

Cover
The illustration on the front cover is by
The Attic Publishing Co.

CONTENTS

Chapter One: Sex and Violence on TV

What are the children watching?	1
New head of film censors vows porn crackdown	3
Sex, violence, and so to bed	4
Violence on television in Britain	5
Sex on TV	6
Research and monitoring	8
Does anyone really believe they'll tackle TV violence?	10
Violence, pornography and the media	11
In the US a new 'chip' will allow parents to censor TV. Could it work here?	14
Lost innocence of the TV children	16
Violence	17
TV and violence	19
Parents advised to vet TV viewing for the young	20
How to comment or complain	22
This kind of violence isn't up our street say viewers	23
Opinion divided over effect of video violence	24
Children and young persons	25
A parent's guide to computer and video games	26

Chapter Two: Classification and Censorship

Classification issues	28
A parent's guide to video classification	30
Children like violence, as long as it only fiction	31
New film censor pledges review of violence in videos and games	32
Censored – violent videos ban for young offenders	33
Video statistics	34
Censors claim the public is ready for more explicit videos	34
Ratings plan for Internet sparks censorship fears	35
Press freedom groups protest Internet censorship	36
Silencing the net	37
Net porn to get X-rating	38
Censor sensibilities	39
Europe's Internet puzzle	40
Additional resources	41
Index	42
Web site information	43
Acknowledgements	44

Introduction

Censorship is the twenty-seventh volume in the series:
Issues. The aim of this series is to offer up-to-date
information about important issues in our world.

Censorship looks at the issues of sex and violence on
TV and the roles of film classification and censorship.

The information comes from a wide variety of sources
and includes:
Government reports and statistics
Newspaper reports and features
Magazine articles and surveys
Literature from lobby groups
and charitable organisations.

It is hoped that, as you read about the many aspects
of the issues explored in this book, you will critically
evaluate the information presented. It is important
that you decide whether you are being presented
with facts or opinions. Does the writer give a biased
or an unbiased report? If an opinion is being expressed,
do you agree with the writer?

Censorship offers a useful starting-point for those
who need convenient access to information about
the many issues involved. However, it is only a
starting-point. At the back of the book is a list of
organisations which you may want to contact for
further information.

*****

What are the children watching?

What every parent should know

Children today are exposed to more violence on the screen than ever before. By 'screen' we mean television, videos, films and computer games as well as the Internet.

With such a wide choice of channels and round-the-clock viewing available to children, and with many teenagers having TVs in their bedrooms, parents are finding it harder to control what their children are watching. While television and other media offer exciting, positive opportunities for learning and entertainment, they can also have negative influences, especially on a young audience.

Research has not yet either proved, or disproved, the link between screen violence and violent behaviour in children. However, the NSPCC believes that it is best to err on the side of caution and that parents and carers should take steps to monitor what their children are watching.

This information looks at the effect that violent or disturbing images on the screen may have on children's behaviour and emotional well-being. It also offers practical advice to help parents and carers to:
- assess the suitability of TV programmes, films and videos for children, according to their age and maturity
- protect children from screen images which may be harmful or disturbing
- be aware of the controls and regulations which exist to help adults make the right decisions
- teach children positive viewing habits from an early age.

This information does not cover the subject of sex or sexual violence on the screen. This issue will be included in a new booklet which the NSPCC is planning to produce.

Is screen violence harmful?
The question 'Is screen violence harmful?' has been the subject of much debate.

Some research does show that children who are frequently exposed to violent images are more likely to:
- copy what they see and behave violently themselves,
- learn the message that violence is a normal and acceptable part of everyday life, or
- become more timid and fearful of the world around them.

Other research shows that:
- screen violence has little effect on children's behaviour,
- violent behaviour in children can be a result of many influences in their lives, not just one.

Even after 30 years of research, it is still not possible to prove that watching violence on the screen encourages violent behaviour in children. However, a Government review concluded:

'There is some evidence to support the commonsense view that videos do have some corrupting influence upon the young which may lead some vulnerable children into crime.'
Home Affairs Committee 1994

What do parents think?
There is growing concern, especially among parents, about how screen violence might be influencing children. These are some of the issues parents raised in a recent survey.

'It has an impact on children and those who can't think about right or wrong. Younger children can be influenced easily – they are vulnerable.'

'There's far too much violence. It shows all the things you tell them not to do.'

'I don't like screen violence, but it doesn't harm him because he's well balanced.'

'Young children copy violence on TV.'

'The trouble is, so many children have got televisions in their bedrooms these days, so you put them to bed and they watch it anyway.'

'Television reflects the changes that are taking place in society, but it doesn't influence them.'

'TV can't be blamed for the world's evils. Parental role is what matters.'

'TV is not as important an influence as parents.'

In the survey many parents said they tended to ignore film and video classifications and the 9pm television 'watershed' (the time after which TV channels may show programmes which are not considered suitable for children):

'They watch after the watershed in their own rooms. I don't know what – it seems a lot to me but I'm not really worried.'

What the children say . . .

This is what some children said in a recent survey when asked about screen violence and how they feel about it.

'My little brother jumped off a wall after seeing a kick-boxer film. He's only six.'

'There is more violence and that on the news . . . I think it affects people more . . . I worry about it.'

'Just because there are bad things happening on TV it doesn't necessarily mean that people will do these in real life. And vice versa. People won't go out to try to save the world just because it was on telly.'

'If TV influences your friends, say your best mates, then it influences you. You do what your mates want you to do a lot of the time. You have to keep up with everyone else.'

'When Bruce Willis blows away a load of villains, it's a laugh. You know it's not real. I think violence in EastEnders is more shocking because it's more real life. It's not silly or glossy.'

Remember that each child is an individual. It is difficult to predict which images may frighten or disturb a child. An image that appears completely harmless to one child may frighten or upset another child of the same age. The scenes or characters that you think your children will be upset by may not affect them at all. And the ones that you think are harmless might be the ones that do cause them upset.

What can you do?

- Take the issue of screen violence seriously. You know your children better than anyone, so it's your responsibility to protect them from images that may be harmful or disturbing.
- Remember, your attitude to violence will directly affect your child's. The way violent images affect children often depends on whether an adult is present to condemn the violence or comment on what is happening.
- Try to build on your child's own ways of dealing with the fear, if possible. Children tend to apply their own logic to images or characters they don't like. For example, they might decide that the monster is made of cloth and is therefore not a threat at all. They might simply close their eyes, look away or ask you to watch the scene with them.
- Ask your friends what videos they allow their children to watch and how they help their children cope with scenes which may upset them.
- If you use a babysitter or have a childminder, make it clear to them what you allow your children to watch on screen, and what you do not want them to watch. You may also want to give them this information to read.

How do screen images affect children?

Television and screen images can play a big part in shaping our children's understanding of the world. The way in which children respond to stories and images they see on the screen, especially frightening or violent ones, will depend mainly on their age and maturity.

The information below is a guide to the different stages of a child's development, showing to what extent children can understand and relate to screen images. It also gives ideas on how you can help them to make sense of what they see. Remember that it is only a guide to children's development. All children are different.

Research tells us that the more children think and talk about what they see on the screen, the better they are able to cope.

Under-5s

Under-5s generally:
- Have an increasing interest in the screen, and like to watch favourite scenes and characters over and over again.
- Develop specific technical skills such as how the controls work.
- Are able to put a video and other objects, such as toast, into the video recorder.
- Have trouble following and remembering the story.
- Tend to focus on exciting images with a lot of movement and sound, such as commercials.
- Are likely to copy actions seen on the screen.
- Do not yet understand cause and effect.
- Cannot easily tell the difference between fantasy and reality. Tend to see cartoon characters as real, for example.

What can you do?
- Supervise what your child watches as much as you can. This age group usually can't tell the difference between real and fictional violence, and tend to copy behaviour they see. It is not always easy to be with children when they are watching television, or to know what screen images might upset them. If you are popping out of the room, check what they're watching and keep the remote control out of reach.
- Also look out for any behaviour they may be copying from the screen that could be violent or dangerous either to themselves or others.

6-9 year olds

Children of this age generally:
- Understand and remember the story.
- Still find it difficult to tell the difference between fantasy and reality. May see cartoon characters as fantasy and laugh, but may also think that the message 'violence wins' is acceptable.

What can you do?
- Talk to your children about what they like to watch and why. Listen to their views. Allow them to describe their feelings towards characters and stories and ask them to tell you what they think is happening. Ask them how they feel about violent scenes. Are they scared, worried, sad or excited?

10-16 year olds

Children of this age generally:
- Can tell the difference between fact and fiction.
- Understand and remember the content of stories.
- Are disturbed by material based on fact, such as news items or 'true-life' soaps. Feel that it could happen to them, their family or near to where they live.
- Are likely to absorb the message that 'violence wins' from heroes in action movies.
- Feel protective towards younger siblings and children being exposed to screen violence.

What can you do?
- Encourage your child to discuss programmes or films with you. As children get older and more independent, it is not so easy to supervise what they're watching. Taking an interest in your child's choices will help form positive viewing habits from an early age. And don't forget to ask which videos they will be watching when visiting their friends.

• The above is an extract from *Screen Violence – What every parent should know*, produced by the NSPCC. See page 41 for address details.

New head of film censors vows porn crackdown

By Dan Glaister, Arts Correspondent

A row over the future of the British Board of Film Classification was resolved yesterday when Jack Straw, the Home Secretary, announced the appointment of Andreas Whittam Smith as the body's new president.

Mr Whittam Smith, a co-founder of the *Independent* newspaper, was appointed to replace the Earl of Harewood. Earlier this month it emerged Mr Straw had vetoed the appointment of Lord Birkett, a BBFC vice president, as the new chairman.

The row between the Home Office and the BBFC follows a dispute over what was seen as a unilateral relaxation of guidelines on sexually explicit and violent films by James Ferman, the chief censor.

The difference centred on the passing of two sexually explicit films by the BBFC as R18, which means they can be sold in licensed sex shops. But after the films had been passed, Customs and Excise warned the distributors that they faced prosecution. The confusion was blamed on Mr Ferman, but was seen as symptomatic of the unaccountability of the board.

Mr Whittam Smith said: 'I am very uncomfortable about these videos. One of the first things I would like to look at is the issue of pornography. You simply can't have a situation where videos which police could seize are licensed. I am more worried about video than film. In cinemas there is a natural gatekeeping mechanism and it is unlikely an 11-year-old can get in to see an 18-certificate film.'

The argument between the board and the Home Office rumbled on yesterday as the Home Office demanded publication of the BBFC's annual report for 1996. A Home Office spokesman said: 'We have been chasing them to produce their report for some time. We're aware that it's overdue.'

The BBFC is run by the film industry and operates a voluntary system of classification. It has a statutory duty under the 1994 Video Recordings Act to classify videos and video games.

Mr Whittam Smith said: 'I am honoured to be asked to undertake such an important task. One of the purposes of the board is to help parents protect their children from material which might harm them. I shall have that objective constantly in mind.'

He said he would look at three areas of the BBFC's work. These would be an internal review of its workings, taking into account staff opinions; an examination of the research into the connection between violent films and the behaviour of young offenders; and consultation with various interest groups.

'I am aware of the suggestions that the work of the board is too secretive,' he said. 'I hope to see if we can find some method of conducting meetings around the country.'

Sex, violence, and so to bed

It's true – children are staying up to watch unsuitable television programmes. Tom Kemp feels a strange kind of relief

A survey published this week has resoundingly confirmed what millions of parents already strongly suspected: that the British broadcasters' code for shielding children from sex and violence on television has been based on a wild fantasy.

The 25-year-old fantasy is that the nation's children – teeth scrubbed, hair brushed, prayers said – are all tucked up in bed and drifting off to sleep by 9pm.

It may be that, once upon a time, every child had a fixed bedtime in the early or mid-evening. But, as this week's survey by Market Assessment Publications (MAP) has so convincingly found, that golden age – if it ever existed – is no more.

The finding that no fewer than seven out of 10 children nowadays, including almost all the over-13s, regularly watch television after the 9pm watershed must have come as a great relief to most parents. Yes, we always had a feeling that we were not the only ones whose efforts to impose an immovable bedtime had utterly failed. But, gosh, it was nice to know for sure.

My wife and I set out with the best of intentions to see that our children were in bed by a given time every evening. It would be good for them, but it would also be good for us.

The rule would be completely inflexible, and there would be no right of appeal. After a while, it would be accepted by the children as a fact of life and obeyed automatically. In our perfectly regulated household, the days would belong to the children, but the late evenings would be for the grown-ups.

That was the theory. It is hard to remember, at this distance of 10 years, when the policy started to go wrong, but I think it was right from the beginning. As a baby, our eldest preferred to sleep during the day and to bawl during the night. We became used to having him up with us late in front of the television, and he became used to being with us.

There was a brief period when his sleep pattern began to settle down, but by that time there was a second baby as nocturnally active as the first. The first began to think it unfair that his younger brother was allowed to be up while he was in bed. We weakened. The bedtime rule never had a chance to become properly established.

Now there are four boys, and the household that was to be so perfectly regulated is as chaotic as British Rail during a signalmen's strike. The two-year-old never sleeps, except in the car and at odd moments in the small hours.

The four-year-old arrives home shattered from school in the afternoon, crashes out on the sofa and begins to come to life again in the

early evening. The nine-year-old stays up because his older brother stays up.

His older brother stays up because once too often in the past, when he begged to watch a special programme, we said: 'Oh, all right – just this once.' Anarchy rules in our household – just as it rules, according to the MAP survey, all over the land.

And so there we sit, with one or more of the children, feeling faintly uncomfortable about all the bloodshed, the cursing and the heavy grunting flesh on television. Should we switch it off? Then we tell ourselves: why make an issue of it and further excite their interest? Anyway, we want to watch.

The MAP survey highlights the absurdity of the Independent Television Commission's antics over the years. There the great and good sit, solemnly processing complaints that some risqué scene or dirty word has been broadcast before that fantasy 'watershed', when all those fantasy children are in bed. Meanwhile, real children remain glued to the set until well into the night.

Even if there were no such things as video recorders, even if four out of 10 under-17s did not have television sets in their own rooms, there would be only one way to ensure that children saw nothing unsuitable on television. And that would be to broadcast nothing unsuitable for them, at any hour of the day or night.

Perhaps there are a few perfect parents whose children do have a set bedtime, and who bless the 9pm watershed. Perhaps it is possible to impose a fixed bedtime on the young. But if there is a way to do it, I haven't found it. And I find it comforting to know that I am in the vast majority.

Violence on television in Britain

Summary and conclusions

This research indicates that, amongst most viewers, there appears to be relatively little spontaneous, that is to say unprompted, concern about violence on TV.

Significantly, many do not think that there is much violence on TV nowadays. In part, this reflects self-censorship with those who do not like watching extreme violence on TV avoiding these programmes. But it also indicates that most are confining their definition of violence to more extreme portrayals.

Whilst precise definitions of violence tend to be very individual and personal, most seem to distinguish between violent acts that are more graphic, realistic and shocking, and those which are less real, less graphic and generally less perturbing. This means that many people do not see the more slapstick violence of Bond movies, old-fashioned Westerns/war movies, cartoon, etc., as at all violent.

This calls into question the relevance to most viewers of clinical definitions of violence as used in the past for content analyses. It is observable that a definition of violence that incorporates a more subjective dimension is more relevant, e.g.: 'Violence on TV is any scene which shows one or more people hurting or harming another person or people. It is less acceptable as it becomes more graphic, gratuitous or sadistic'.

A range of attitudes towards violence on TV emerges. At one extreme, a minority, mainly female, and often elderly, clearly dislikes programmes containing a high quotient of graphic violence. At the other, a male minority seems to have a very high threshold of tolerance for extreme violence. In a middle category are the majority of viewers who have an upper limit of some

Independent Television Commission

kind. They find very graphic, vivid portrayals of fictional or real life violence off-putting.

There are indications that people are more likely to be sensitive to violence if they identify with or have great sympathy for the victim, e.g. rape victims, children and animals.

Levels of acceptance of violence on TV are strongly related to age and gender. Younger respondents are largely unconcerned about fictional, 'unreal', albeit gory portrayals of violence. There is a possibility that a generation that has grown up with graphic violence may have become somewhat desensitised. The older segments, especially over-55s, are often quite resistant to violence on TV, finding much of it too graphic and vivid.

In general, men are inclined to display more tolerance of violence on TV than women. They accept most violent portrayals as long as they are in context and at the appropriate time.

Women express more reservations about violence on TV – but a sizeable minority watches and enjoys programmes which contain some violent elements. There are hints that the suspense generated by the threat of violence may increase the excitement of some viewing. Whilst women reject portrayals of sexual violence against women, they also seem to have a lower overall threshold of acceptance of graphic violence than men.

There are indications that feelings about the acceptability of violent portrayals are quite subjective and could relate to factors such as:

- relevance to the plot;
- involvement with the victim;
- whether they feel the victim deserved it;
- the degree of inequality between victim and perpetrator;
- the degree of brutality shown;
- whether the camera dwells on the violence/invites the audience to revel in it;
- how graphic the violence is.

Clearly personal sensitivity to and interest in violence is also an influential factor, as is the time when the programme is shown.

Invited to map selected examples of violent scenes, viewers develop the following main categories:

- 'Fantasy/harmless' – James Bond
- 'Historical/Educational' – *Sharpe*
- 'Everyday family drama' – *Casualty*
- 'Real life' – boxing, the News
- 'Adult (unacceptable) drama' – rape scene in *London Bridge*

For men, all these categories were suitable for TV viewing subject to appropriate schedules and warnings. Women drew the line at 'Adult (unacceptable) drama'.

- The above is an extract from a news release from the Independent Television Commission. See page 41 for address details.

© Independent Television Commission (ITC)

Sex on TV

Information from the National Viewers' and Listeners' Association

Storytelling, and listening to stories, is an intrinsic part of our human nature. Morality tales, with good triumphing over evil, are one tradition which is alive and well. The love story is another. The classic romance, in which the hero and the heroine meet, fall in love and then have to decide whether to get married or not, and resolve their other relationships, is as old as time.

We all identify with love stories and enjoy them at different levels of sophistication depending on our taste and maturity. In the absence of any moral guidance, we also draw on them as a resource to help us work out how we should conduct our own lives. In short, we need them.

The issue, then, is not with the love story itself, but how it is told on TV and film and video. We recognise that there is a clear difference between the images each of us finds erotic, and images which are pornographic. What we find erotic is highly personal and can be quite neutral in its own right, like the face of our loved one or our favourite TV celebrity. Or it can be an image which is intended to titillate us, like the footage of semi-naked bodies shown at tea time on *Bay Watch*! Either way, we do not say such things are pornographic in themselves!

But graphic sex on TV *is* pornographic. It undermines respect for human dignity – hence it is pornographic in the literal sense – because we become desensitised by it. Many people – of all faiths and none – say they find the all-out portrayal of sex on TV offensive, because its deliberate portrayal assumes the audience is without imagination.

What about nudity on TV? This is an important issue too. As a guideline, the state of undress that we accept in the street is what is appropriate on our screens. TV is a public arena, not a private one.

Two key events in the 1960s had a major impact on the way we discuss these things. The first key event was the ineptly handled obscenity trial of *Lady Chatterley's Lover*, D. H. Lawrence's least impressive book. This ended in failure for the Crown and the ridiculing of the new Obscene Publications Act. The second key event was the end of official censorship in the theatre at around the same time.

The new 'permissive' atmosphere of the 1960s meant that writers, producers and directors could reveal more of the characters' sexual activities, liaisons and misadventures, without risk of prosecution owing to badly worded law.

The lack of moral leadership gave people the chance to think about changing attitudes to sex

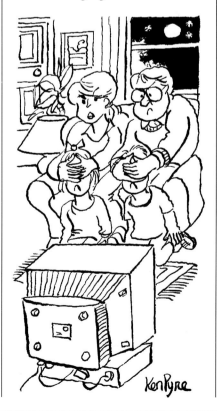

before marriage. But in the 1960s, portrayal of the sex act itself remained largely confined to 'porn' films, the preserve of seedy men in dirty raincoats and cheeky schoolboys furtively venturing down the back streets of Soho and elsewhere.

In Britain there was still very much a 'seaside postcard' attitude to sex at the cinema. Feature films tended to be suggestive rather than graphically revealing. The audience knew what the characters were up to but we didn't expect to see them doing it. Even in *The Graduate*, what Ben (Dustin Hoffman) did to Mrs Robinson (Anne Bancroft) was mostly left to our imaginations. The sex scene as we know it first reached its current prominence in the 1970s, with a wave of Hollywood directors who started pushing it to new heights of explicitness. And here, in Britain, our directors caught on too knowing that they could also get away with it.

Compare the relative innocence of films like *The Knack (And How To Get It)* or *Georgie Girl*, with the sophistication of *A Touch of Class*, a few short years later, in which George Segal is married with children but is intent on playing around with Glenda Jackson, who is divorced with children. And yet, before they become entangled she asks him if he knows what he is doing. Her attitude suggests that though divorced, she still has a basic concern about breaking up his marriage.

In any case, this sort of thing passed largely unnoticed in Britain at the time. In the 1970s the British Board of Film Censors was justifiably more concerned with the likes of *A Clockwork Orange* and *The Devils*.

Meanwhile playwrights and TV writers flourished in the freer atmosphere of the 1970s. Some would say that Dennis Potter, in particular, made his reputation for pushing back the barriers, following on from the tradition of the 'Plays For Today' of the 1960s – dramas which led to Mary Whitehouse founding the National Viewers' and Listeners' Association.

The impact these TV dramas enjoyed was soon to be eclipsed by the impact of video technology. In the 1980s, with the arrival of the video recorder in four out of five homes, it was suddenly possible to capture all the more explicit films on tape and see them at one's leisure – rewinding and replaying the exciting bits to our heart's content. With the video recorder, suddenly there simply wasn't enough on TV to keep people amused.

So during the 1980s video rental shops and video 'sell-through' arrived on our high streets in a big way. The cinema box office suffered for a while as consumers discovered the convenience of catching up on the recent films at home. (It has caught up since, as people realise the limitations of the small screen.) Digital technology will enable much larger domestic TV screens and sophisticated audio equipment is now available to give cinema-quality stereo sound. With the video retailer effectively acting as the moral guardian, there was a clear difference between what was acceptable on TV and what could have a video release. With such a choice now available – and with so little regulation – ultimately the viewer became even more blasé about sex on TV. And the morality behind it was accepted too!

The films themselves were much 'darker' in tone. The Glenn Close character in *Fatal Attraction*, made in the late 1980s, couldn't care two hoots about breaking up Michael Douglas' marriage after a fling. She was a far cry from the Glenda Jackson character in *A Touch Of Class*, who did care, as we have mentioned.

TV broadcasting also expanded in the 1980s, with the launch of Channel 4, which was given a 'bad boy' manifesto from Day 1. Interestingly the first ads C4 showed were for a brand of videotape! The Government was under pressure to act from National VALA and others, and the result was the formation of

---
*Film censor
or no film censor,
the important point is
that the current TV
regulations are ineffective
in dealing with
sex on TV*
---

the Broadcasting Standards Council. But generally speaking this has taken a lenient view of a worsening situation, which some say has been caused by the Broadcasting Authorities' failure to regulate effectively and contriving Codes of Practice that permit maximum latitude in terms of taste and decency in programmes.

In the 1990s, movies on TV became ever more important in attracting an audience to please the advertisers. Led by Channel 4 the TV companies also became directly involved with film production, so that they could be guaranteed first showing. Some of these films reflected clearly the attitudes of the broadcasters behind them. Channel 4's biggest film production success so far has been *Four Weddings And A Funeral*, a comedy in which the leading character – played by Hugh Grant – is pathologically unable to commit himself to marriage. This attitude, the film tells us in a script full of F-words, is now acceptable!

But *Four Weddings And A Funeral* wasn't the worst of it, by any means. In 1996, James Ferman, the then Director of the British Board of Film Classification, said publicly that he felt helpless to control the nature of the films coming our way from Hollywood – all of which were bound to end up on our TV screens sooner or later after their cinema release. Sadly, this remark, and his further remark that we must hope that Hollywood wakes up with a conscience, brought no suggestion that the Government might intervene.

Film censor or no film censor, the important point is that the current TV regulations are ineffective in dealing with sex on TV.

The BBC's Royal Charter, governing BBC1, BBC2, and any other 'narrowcast' channels the BBC may operate in the near future, is largely powerless to temper the more bold creative brains and commissioners of programmes. And the independent contractors can see equally clearly that the Broadcasting Act can do nothing directly to curtail their excesses.

In the late 1990s the wheel is turning still further, with the arrival of Channel 5, numerous satellite and cable TV channels and the digital expansion that is in prospect. How on earth can all these channels be controlled and breaches of good taste and decency redressed? No-one can possibly watch them all and see all the programmes. We are faced with a new situation which has arisen without any real public or parliamentary debate: the onus for maintaining standards is shifting away from the broadcasting authorities to ordinary viewers and listeners who will be expected to write and complain every time offence has been caused. Since no objective standards of good taste and decency seem to apply the only measure of dissatisfaction will be the number of protests from the public received by the broadcasting authorities. And the outcome of such protestation, as is well known, is at best uncertain and most often rejected.

It is true that the police still crack down on the really obscene videos. But when it comes to the ever bolder 'run-of-the-mill' sex scenes shown on TV, the bemused audience is presented with two choices – like it and keep watching, or lump it and turn off. We say that's ridiculous. We believe that an overhaul of the Obscene Publications Act is long overdue – the only legal measure left to enable action against sex on TV – to strengthen and update the law effectively.

• The above is an extract from *Television and Sex*, produced by the National Viewers' and Listeners' Association. See page 41 for address details.

Research and monitoring

Monitoring report 5

Communications Research Group, Aston University; Network Research & Marketing Ltd

Monitoring Report 5, to be published in 1997, provides an analysis of trends in public attitudes towards issues within the remit as well as a review of data from five years of television content analyses. Key findings from the annual opinion poll, audience monitoring panels and content analysis relating to television in 1996 are presented below.

Annual opinion poll results
Scheduling

Most respondents (91%) claimed to be aware of the watershed with eighty-one per cent placing it correctly at 9.00pm. There was less certainty about its timing at weekends, when one in five respondents thought it differed from weekdays.

Three-quarters of respondents thought parents should take most responsibility for what their children viewed before 9.00pm and this increased to ninety-four per cent after the watershed.

Of those who said that broadcasters should take special care about the material they transmitted, respondents were most likely to mention violence (79%), followed by sexual explicitness (59%) and bad language (50%). Violence was also the most frequently mentioned issue by parents (82%). However, they were marginally more concerned about bad language than the depiction of sexual activity (mentioned by 51% and 47% of parents respectively).

Information about programmes

The 1995 BSC Annual Review revealed that transmission time was seen as the key indicator of content. Timing was considered crucial and

69% of respondents considered that the watershed would be necessary even if programmes carried a pre-transmission warning.

Of the additional information available, respondents appeared to find on-screen information more useful than information carried in listings magazines or programme guides.

64% of respondents considered there was 'too much' violence on television, an increase from 57% the previous year. This figure marks a return to the levels previously recorded. Age remains a key demographic variable in all the responses, with older people more likely to say there was 'too much' violence than younger people. Women were also more likely to say there was 'too much' than men.

When respondents were questioned further about the single

Issues of concern

**Viewing events perceived to contain significant violence, bad language and sex.
July 1996 – April 1997**

Source: Broadcasting Standards Commission

issue which caused them most concern, nearly two in three (65%) mentioned violence. Twenty-two per cent mentioned bad language and a further ten per cent mentioned the depiction of sex.

Levels of offence

Most respondents with children (90%) said they had watched television with their offspring and over half (55%) said they had had occasion to switch off when doing so. Nearly half (47%) mentioned violence as the reason. A similar proportion (41%) mentioned sexual explicitness, particularly in drama and films.

Significantly fewer respondents (38%) said they had switched off or changed channel because they had been personally disgusted by something. Bad language, violence and sexual explicitness were mentioned by 35%, 32% and 29% of the sample respectively.

Few respondents (5%) had ever turned off the radio because of personal disgust.

Audience monitoring panel results

When respondents in the annual monitoring exercise were asked about the levels of violence, bad language and sexual activity in programmes they had viewed, they were more likely to mention significant levels of violence. However, the overall levels were low as in previous years.

This means that across a two-week period, respondents noted significant violence in only 3 of 44 programmes they watched on average, bad language in 1.6 programmes and explicit sex in 1.4 programmes.

The watershed made a clear difference, with the majority of incidents in each category occurring after 9.00pm

When asked if these incidents were justifiable or not, only 1% of pre-watershed viewing was considered unjustifiable and this was true of 3 to 4% of post-watershed viewing. The table opposite gives the percentages of incidents that were marked as containing significant levels of bad language, sexual activity or violence and whether they were considered to be justified or not within their context and at the time they occurred.

The data reveals a similar trend to previous years with violence more likely to be justified within its context than either bad language or sexual activity. Indeed the data shows a further 6% rise in the numbers of unjustified incidents of bad language in pre-watershed programmes compared to the previous year. For all incidents respondents were more likely to judge their pre-watershed portrayal more severely than if the incident occurred after the watershed.

Content analysis results

For the fifth year running, the Communications Research Group have noted the nature and amount of bad language and the depictions of sexual activity as well as the representation of key minority groups in programmes over a specified period.

The sample reported here was made up of two composite weeks in 1996. All programmes broadcast between 17.30 hours and midnight on the four terrestrial channels and those between 18.00 hours and midnight on four satellite channels (Sky Movies, The Movie Channel, Sky One and UK Gold) were analysed.

Bad language

Four out of ten programmes (45%) in the terrestrial sample contained a total of 2,239 incidents of bad language. In the sample of satellite programmes 81% of the programmes contained a total of 1,792 incidents of bad language. In both terrestrial and satellite samples the majority of incidents were words from a religious origin with many coded as mild. These occurred generally in fiction and films. On

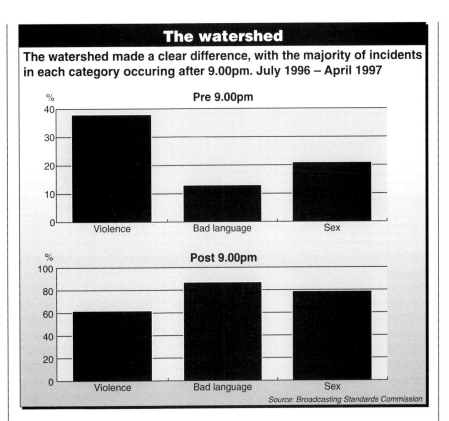

The watershed

The watershed made a clear difference, with the majority of incidents in each category occuring after 9.00pm. July 1996 – April 1997

Source: Broadcasting Standards Commission

terrestrial television the sample revealed that 40 instances of bad language within 15 programmes were masked or bleeped. Many, but not all, of these related to pre-watershed programmes.

Bad language was more prevalent in both samples after 9.00 pm, indicating observance of the watershed. On terrestrial television 140 programmes (36% of all pre-watershed programmes) included some bad language, most were words from a religious origin or words classified as mild. There were no incidents of 'serious' bad language noted in this sample. After 9.00 pm, 152 programmes (58% of all post watershed programmes) contained bad language and 9% of the instances were classified as 'serious'. Bad language was most prevalent between 10pm and 11pm.

Satellite television film channels operate a 'double watershed' policy (in which films that would be classified by the British Board of Film Classification as '15' can be shown at 8.00pm and those classified as '18' can be shown from 10.00pm). Of the films in which the language was coded as 'serious', three began at 8.00pm, the remainder at 10pm or later. No other programmes contained any 'serious' bad language before the watershed.

Sexual activity

Nearly one in five programmes (19%) on terrestrial television contained a total of 267 scenes of sexual activity, a similar proportion to the previous year. Within the satellite sample, this figure doubled to two in five programmes. However, the majority of scenes were inexplicit with 'kissing with sexual intent' being the most common activity in over three-quarters of all cases. This was true of scenes both before and after the watershed. In most cases, across both samples, the sexual activity could have been anticipated from the storyline or narrative.

Nearly half the scenes of sexual activity took place within the content of married or established relationships. Very few scenes showed any sexual violence. In the terrestrial sample, this was found in only three programmes and in only five in the satellite sample.

Scenes of nudity were rare in pre-watershed programming. On terrestrial television, none was shown in an adult context before 9.00pm and on satellite television, one-quarter were in the context of sexual activity.

• The above information is from the Broadcasting Standards Commission. See page 41 for address details.

© Broadcasting Standards Commission

Does anyone really believe they'll tackle TV violence?

Because I don't. By Milton Sulman, TV critic and programme producer

The murder in 1993 of two-year-old James Bulger by two ten-year-old boys brought a quantum shift in public opinion about the influence of TV on the young.

These boys had undoubtedly watched a great deal of television, much of it violent. Something must be done, everyone agreed.

But it needed the passion and eloquence of Frances Lawrence, widow of the murdered headmaster Philip, to galvanise the debate. In her plea for a new moral agenda, she included a call for higher standards on TV. Everyone nodded sagely and leaders of the main political parties and the Anglican, Catholic and Jewish faiths joined in.

Trailing behind, as they always are when confronted with a spasm of anger by their viewers, were the broadcasters. Pious assertions by the BBC and Independent Television followed, with announcements that they will do their utmost to clean up their schedules.

The BBC this week issued a 'charter', filled with promises. They will, for example, abide more strictly to their 9pm watershed. But isn't this precisely what they have been saying for decades, whenever they have been challenged about how contemptuously they treat the guidelines?

The ITC pathetically defends itself by protesting that only a small number of viewers – 11 per cent – complain about violence. They blame their problems on parents who do not enforce the watershed in their homes.

Inevitably, politicians have come in on the act. Tom Sackville, a Home Office Minister, has castigated video producers and Virginia Bottomley, the Heritage Secretary, has arranged a summit meeting with broadcasters to demand a reduction in the levels of violence to protect children from 'corrupting material'.

Forgive me but I'm afraid I've heard it all before. As a TV critic and producer of programmes. I have been passionately involved in the whole television and violence debate for more than 25 years. I have written books, dozens of newspaper articles, taken part in endless discussions on TV and radio about the problem.

I have had interviews with Home Secretaries, leaders of political parties and media bosses. Everyone professes concern. But has any serious action ever been taken to curb such TV? Of course not. The very little that has been done has proved ineffectual or half-hearted.

Each new chairman of the BBC when he takes his post vows that he will look seriously at the question of too much violence on the box. So Sir Christopher Bland, the latest chairman at the BBC, agrees that the corporation has a part to play in

'raising the moral standards of the country'. And what will happen? Nothing, I regret to say.

The most chilling of recent crime statistics reveals that more than 3,000 violent crimes (muggings, woundings, assaults) were committed by children between 10 and 14, many by girls. No sane person can deny that violence on television has played a large part in this frightening escalation.

The first ripples of concern about the impact of TV violence became evident in America after the assassinations of President Kennedy, his brother Senator Edward Kennedy and Martin Luther King. A President's National Commission on Violence examined the facts and concluded in 1969 that violence in TV programmes 'has adverse effects on audiences – particularly child audiences'.

The report was brushed aside by the producers of violent films and videos, confident in their belief that the provisions for Free Speech in the American constitution would protect them from any government action. There was soon a flood of violent films from Hollywood such as those by Peckinpah and the spaghetti Westerns starring a murderous Clint Eastwood.

TV competed with this entertainment by showing the most violent of these films on their schedules. Satellite and cable TV, dominated by the Rupert Murdoch channels, even out-did Hollywood in the ugliness and mayhem of their product.

In 1979 a most significant study was published. A seven-year study of 1,565 London boys, conducted by Dr William Belson, concluded there was as much evidence to link TV with adolescent violence as smoking with lung cancer.

Since then, scientific evidence has mounted.

Through watching violent programmes three to four hours a day from the ages of six to 14, TV has become a conditioning factor in children's upbringing. It is more potent than the influence of their teachers, parents or priests, teaching them that violence is a normal ingredient of everyday life. Good guys – sheriffs, cops, private detectives, FBI, MI5 – use violence as much as villains.

TV sets and videos in children's bedrooms are now commonplace, even in apparently responsible households. Children can defy all watershed guidelines. The results of this battering of young minds is, I believe, more harmful in its overall effects than nicotine, asbestos or petrol fumes.

America is as worried as we are in Britain about the problem and is starting to take steps. The introduction of the V-chip in every new set was promised by President Clinton, undoubtedly influenced by findings in 1993 of a Congressional Committee headed by Senator Simon. Speaking to the heads of the major TV companies, he said: 'Since 1961 there has been a perception that violence on the screen added to violence in our society. Today we know that is a fact. The research is just overwhelming. There is no question that it is a causal factor.' None of his listeners dared contradict him.

The V-chip will offer parents hope of blotting out programmes they deem unsuitable for their children. The mass boycott of particularly violent programmes could seriously hit the ratings and profits of the companies.

Advertisers would not be keen to have their products associated with such a protest and pressure on the companies to find alternative programmes would be irresistible.

It could help us here too though there are doubts whether those households which most need the V-chip would actually utilise it.

More radical would be for the Prime Minister and Mrs Bottomley to consider sanctions. If there was a real will to reduce the volume of gratuitous violence on television, they could threaten the BBC with the loss of their monopoly licence fee. TV companies could be told that they would lose their franchises if they did not abide by their promises.

Not that I am optimistic. As I said, we have been here before.

Violence, pornography and the media

Information from The Maranatha Community, a movement of Christians in all the main churches

Behaviour on the screen is replicated in real life
The Royal Society for the Prevention of Accidents has published the results of a survey involving 91 headteachers of primary schools. 91% confirmed that there was a link between violent television pro-grammes and aggressive behaviour in schools. 79% said there had been incidents of injuries linked to copy-cat play and gave the following instances: 'aggressive high kicking', 'kick jumping, violent and threatening behaviour', 'teeth lost/loosened, bruising', 'one nine-year-old broke another boy's arm by holding it and knee dropping onto it'. In view of the kind of aggressive behaviour exhibited, it is highly significant that no less than

52% mentioned the television programme *Power Rangers* by name.

A TV wrestler known for wrapping a python around his neck before bouts was one of toddler Jake Terney's idols. But when the two-year-old tried to copy the gimmick of namesake 'Jake the Snake' Roberts, it ended in tragedy. As the boy played in his bedroom at home, he wrapped a loose electric cable twice round his neck and strangled himself. His father, David, said his son, who had a quilt cover decorated with pictures of wrestlers including American Roberts and a python, would imitate his idol by putting belts around his neck.

Basic Instinct, a sex thriller, prompted a woman to lure a sailor

into a Portsmouth side street and stab him in the stomach. Vanessa Ballantyne, aged 41, watched the controversial smash hit film on video, then grabbed a five-inch kitchen knife and went looking for a man to stab.

Stop or my mum will shoot, an action comedy video starring Sylvester Stallone, was watched by a six-year-old girl who then accidentally shot her grandfather dead with his revolver as she copied a scene from the film.

Power Rangers, a children's programme, has prompted copy-cat violence by children in many countries. Staff on one primary school 'have had to stop pupils imitating the karate kicks and arm-swinging of characters from the GMTV *Power Rangers* Show'. (*Manchester Evening News* 3.11.94) In Norway, the children's programme *Power Rangers* had to be withdrawn because of complaints. A link had been suggested between the killing of a little five-year-old girl by her six-year-old friends.

The ITV series *Cracker* featured two characters who were stabbed to death. The Lincoln Coroner, Roger Atkinson, stated at an inquest that the murder of a midwife twelve hours after the broadcasting of this episode could have led to her death. The response of Granada Television was to dismiss the coroner's remarks as 'only his opinion'.

There is now massive public concern about the damage being inflicted by the media.

Opinion Research Business conducted a national opinion survey in June 1996, 61% felt that freedom of expression has gone too far. In answer to the question, 'Do you think the current safeguards to protect children from seeing violence and sex in the media, either through TV or video are too little, too much or about right?', 68% said too little.

- A Gallup Poll presented the question, 'Do you believe that society as a whole is less moral today than it was fifty years ago, or do you not believe that?' The answer was, 'yes, less moral' – 75%, 'no, not less moral' – 17%; 'don't know' – 8%. Of those who answered 'yes', 48% said that television and the media were mostly to blame. (*Daily Telegraph* 5.7.96)

A *Times-Mirror* poll in March 1993 showed that 80% of Americans believe that television now exerts a negative impact on society.

A MORI poll conducted for BBC2's *The Late Show* revealed that two-thirds of the public believed that violence on television is directly linked to anti-social behaviour among children. 66% agreed that watching violence was likely to make children act violently and 76% felt that watching violence made children more likely to accept violence in real life.

The Independent Broadcasting

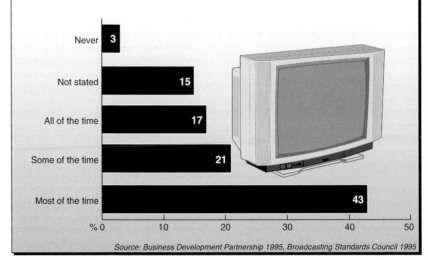

How often do parents know what their children are watching on TV in their bedrooms?

In 39% of households with children, the children have TV sets in their bedrooms. The older the child, the more likely they are to have their own set.

	%
Never	3
Not stated	15
All of the time	17
Some of the time	21
Most of the time	43

Source: Business Development Partnership 1995, Broadcasting Standards Council 1995

Authority commissioned research and dealing with perceptions of TV violence 60% of those interviewed agreed that TV violence gives children the impression that murder occurs daily. 60% agreed that too many programmes on television contain violence.

The British Broadcasting Standards Council's annual survey, compiled from an independent national poll of 1000 adults, an analysis of 544 TV programmes and the responses of a 431-strong audience panel, showed that 57% of viewers believed that there was too much bad language in the programmes. Broadcasters were causing 'particular upset and hurt' by widespread use of potentially blasphemous language such as Jesus Christ, Holy Mother, Christ and Hell. Bad language occurred in nearly half of all terrestrial TV programmes monitored and 80% of those on satellite channels (*Daily Mail*, 12.6.96). Even in 1994 the Annual Report of the BSC reported that there had been a 60% increase about swear words and blasphemy. The BSC had to undertake research following a threefold rise in complaints about standards of taste and decency on radio, mostly on Radio Four. The Deputy Chairwoman of the Council stated that most of the complaints related to bad language and 'explicit sexual activity determined from sound effects'.

The *TV Times* (25th June – 1st

July 1994) reported their special survey in which 59% of parents stated they believed that TV violence encourages criminal behaviour and that 45% of children confused fact and fiction on TV.

Manchester Evening News carried out a survey of readers and 99% voted that there was too much swearing on TV (14.6.96).

What we see on the screen does influence us

During the year ending 31st December, 1995 £1,324 million was spent on TV advertising (Industry Statistics ITC June 1996). Commercial marketing research indicates that buying habits are directly influenced by comparatively short TV advertisements. If this were not so companies would cease advertising. In view of their advertising income television companies cannot deny that the films and advertisements they transmit do directly influence human behaviour. If this were not so, they would lose their advertising revenue.

There is an obsession with violence by film and TV companies.

In an episode of *Casualty* on 13th January 1996 at 8.15pm the BBC broadcast a scene of a man in a balaclava thrusting a broken bottle into the face of a 16-year-old Asian girl outside a school.

The average American 13-year-old has witnessed 8,000 murders and more than 100,000 other acts of violence on TV. This is based on the average child watching 3 hours of television a day (American Psychological Association). The United Kingdom is following the pattern set by the United States.

47 films broadcast on the four terrestrial channels between January and June 1994 were analysed by the National Viewers' and Listeners' Association. These included 244 incidents including fire-arms, 199 violent assaults (60 of them against women), 24 incidents of fire-raising or causing explosions and 21 incidents involving knives. The violence depicted in these films covered the full range of violent acts. These include victims being punched, spat on, dragged by the hair, kicked on the ground, kicked in the stomach, kidneys and genitals. Women are raped and beaten and in one instant a fork put through her cheek. Cruel behaviour depicted, included a man having his hand impaled to a door with scissors, another man having his face smeared with dog faeces. In another instant an ice pick is forced into a victim's throat and also a serrated knife is held at a bound child's throat.

In one typical week on British television there were more than 400 killings screened, 119 woundings and 27 sex attacks on women. Vicious weapons were wielded, foul abusive language was the norm (David Alton).

In *True Lies*, Arnold Schwarzenegger throws a meat-hook into a man's stomach; he hurls a pointed instrument at his torturer which sticks in the man's eye, he breaks a man's neck with his bare hands; and a driver is shot through the head and blood splatters everywhere. This is typical of countless films today.

Satellite movie channels top the TV table of shame. A report by the University of Sheffield found that satellite movie channels showed even more violence than terrestrial channels. The percentage of programmes showing violence on each channel was – Movie Channel – 81%; Sky Movies – 79%; UK Gold – 39%; Sky One – 37%; Channel 4 –

30%; ITV – 29%; BBC1 – 27%, BBC2 23%. (*Daily Mail* 9.8.95)

In a recent Top 60 of video rentals, 35 were exceedingly violent and a further eight were horror. They featured witchcraft, vampirism, serial murder and psychopathic stabbers. (*Carefree Magazine* May 1996)

The film *Heat* is a homage to violence. Almost every scene is dominated by guns – lots of them, and very big ones. All problems are resolved by their use. Such films espouse a culture of violence in which life is cheap and disposable, with random, casual murder the order of the day and victory going to whoever has the biggest gun. It is a world in which civility, rational discourse and the peaceful resolution of differences have no place.

Violence has also invaded the music industry through violent rock and rap singers like WuTang Clan and Onyx, with lyrics about masochism and murder. The techno-punk band 'Nine Inch Nails' produced a video for the song, *Closer*. It is littered with violent imagery. The lead singer is portrayed as decapitated – his head spinning around on a platter.

Heavy metal music, increasingly featured by the media and powerful commercial interests, often glorifies drug use, murder, suicide and

satanism. It debases human relations, degrades sex and is fundamentally aggressive. The pop music industry is playing an increasingly powerful role in TV and sound broadcasting. Obscene and suggestive language is commonplace and Michael Meldred in an article in the *Sunday Times* (28.2.93) states 'Pop music is a mighty industry of staggering global impact that devotes nearly all of its energies to the endless celebration of the raw power of lust'.

The decision of the BBC and the Independent Television Companies to broadcast sex programmes late at night has set a new low standard of broadcasting in this country. Couples speak about intimate sexual encounters in the programmes and the concept of marriage is ridiculed. Promiscuity and sexual deviation are glorified and human relationships are degraded. The broadcasting companies are fully aware that children have access to these programmes and they turn down all complaints.

• The above is an extract from *The truth – about violence, pornography and the media*, produced by The Maranatha Community. See page 41 for address details.

© *The Maranatha Community*

HE WAS SICK OF ALL THE VIOLENCE ON TV SO HE KICKED THE SET IN

Ken Pyne

In the US a new 'chip' will allow parents to censor TV. Could it work here?

What is a V-chip?

Short for Violence Chip, this tiny gadget sits inside a TV set and censors programmes by reading their classification code.

Nifty idea

It was invented by Professor Tim Collings of Simon Fraser University in Vancouver and costs about 60p to fit when the television is being made. The broadcasting industry in Canada is developing a voluntary classification system in conjunction with the chip with the aim of controlling violence in children's programmes such as *Mighty Morph*.

Is it spreading?

A mandatory system may soon be in place in the US. President Clinton signed the Telecommunications Bill this month, which means that from 1998 all new TV sets with a screen size of 13 inches or more sold in America will have to have a V-chip. The only thing that could stop the measure now is a constitutional challenge by civil liberties group – and this is thought unlikely.

Clinton's move is in response to a widespread view in the US that the copious sex and violence on TV are the major reason for the high levels of crime, family breakdown and the perceived decay of American society. According to campaigners for the chip, by the age of 10 the average American child has seen 8,000 murders and 100,000 acts of violence on television.

So is the V-chip coming over here?

Perhaps. This month the European Parliament voted overwhelmingly for the compulsory insertion of V-chips into every new TV set sold in Europe under the Television Without Frontiers directive.

How would it work?

According to amendments proposed by the European Parliament, every programme in Europe would be given a code that could be read by the V-chip, which censors material according to four categories: violence, sex, bad language or an age classification similar to that used for cinema films. This code would be transmitted as a signal along with each programme, and picked up by the V-chip.

Every category could have a rating of one to five, with five the most liberal and one the most restrictive. Parents could instruct the V-chip inside their television to refuse all programmes with a violence level above, say, two, or a sex level above, say, five. When a programme exceeding that level was transmitted, a warning would appear on the TV screen obliterating the picture and switching channels.

What is the drawback?

Civil liberties groups fear it could be used to censor other programmes. Article 19, the international anti-censorship body, worries that such a measure in Europe would allow countries with repressive regimes to censor any TV programme on satellite that comes over their borders.

But there isn't much protection against kids watching violence, is there?

Not a huge amount. The Independent Television Commission relies on the 9pm watershed, which came into being in about 1960. Nothing unsuitable for children should be shown before 9pm, although throughout the evening programmes gradually become more 'suitable' for adults. Film and videos are more closely regulated by being coded according to age by the British Board of Film Classification (BBFC). This started in 1912, although videos have only been classified since 1984.

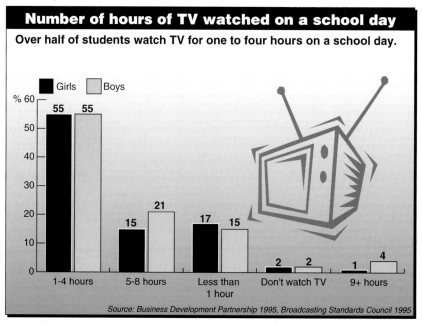

Number of hours of TV watched on a school day

Over half of students watch TV for one to four hours on a school day.

	Girls	Boys
1-4 hours	55	55
5-8 hours	15	21
Less than 1 hour	17	15
Don't watch TV	2	2
9+ hours	1	4

Source: Business Development Partnership 1995, Broadcasting Standards Council 1995

Broadcast warnings of adult material, possibly in the form of symbols in listings pages, are favoured by 94 per cent of people, according to research published in December by the Broadcasting Standards Council.

Of those, 77 per cent thought rape scenes and 'distressing scenes about children' might require a warning, violence was cited by 74 per cent, 'extreme sex' by 71 per cent and bad language by 65 per cent. The BBC's new 10-year charter, to start in April, also has a new 'taste and decency' clause, which legally obliges the BBC's board of governors to act as watchdogs on bad language, gratuitous violence or explicit sex.

And what do the broadcasters think?

They have reacted surprisingly tamely. The official line of the BBC, which lobbied strongly against the new taste and decency clause, is that it is 'watching events with interest'. Granada is more strongly against the notion: a V-chip would play havoc with the audience guarantees it gives to advertisers. The ITV Association also points out the numerous difficulties it could cause, not least to the BBC. 'What's to say someone couldn't V-chip out every programme put out by the BBC and then argue they shouldn't have to pay the licence fee?' asks Ross Biggam, an ITVA European Affairs executive.

There are technical difficulties, too?

If the European Parliament makes it law, the idea is that a Europe-wide body would set the European standard for each tolerance level. The problem is that the 15 member states are highly unlikely to agree on what constitutes a dangerous level of sex or violence. What might offend an Irish housewife is unlikely to shock a Danish student.

Even if the standards could be set on a national rather than a European basis, who would do it? Would it be for the regulators, the Government, the broadcasters, or a quango? How would they agree? It's fraught with difficulty.

Latest time allowed to watch TV on a school day

A survey found that over 50% of boys and girls watch TV after 9pm when programmes considered unsuitable for children may be viewed.

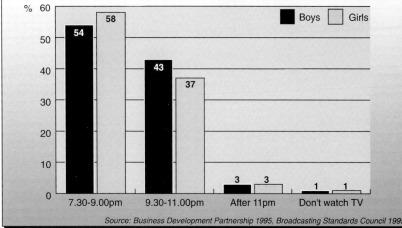

Boys | Girls

	7.30-9.00pm	9.30-11.00pm	After 11pm	Don't watch TV
Boys	54	43	3	1
Girls	58	37	3	1

Source: Business Development Partnership 1995, Broadcasting Standards Council 1995

And there are all sorts of other problems

One is that, if the V-chip becomes mandatory, its effects will not be felt for years – the average life-cycle of a television set is some two decades, so it would be a slow business making the V-chip widely accessible. Mr Biggam of the ITVA points out it would be unfair on homes without children. They would have to fork out – admittedly perhaps not that much – for more expensive TV sets. 'It's similar to making everyone fit a child's seat-belt: a good idea if you have a young child, but fairly pointless for everyone else,' Mr Biggam says.

The point is, will it save the moral health of our kids?

Well, possibly; possibly not. Research shows that when parents buy new TV sets they tend to sling their old ones into their children's bedrooms. In other words, all the V-chipped sets will be in the sitting room and the uncensored ones will be exactly where they shouldn't be.

Kids are also highly computer-literate. Even if you censor television watching, the real bogey has arguably become the Internet, which proffers mind-boggling levels of porn for anyone who cares to browse its 'news-groups' or the World Wide Web.

It is also worth remembering that a comprehensive study published in August by Sheffield University (on behalf of the ITC and BBC) found that violence accounted for just 1 per cent of airtime on terrestrial and satellite television in Britain, and that incidents of violence on the four terrestrial channels had nearly halved since 1986.

Research also shows that people are often most upset by the violence shown on the news, because they are less able to stand back from it. If this is censored by parents too, what implications would that have for TV's important role in educating children about international affairs?

Sounds as if any move to introduce it here would provoke a lot of controversy?

Yes. But it is unlikely to come to this country in the near future as a result of the European initiative, which is likely to get lost in lots of horse trading. It has come about in the US because of the power of the American moral right. Unlike many European countries, America's televisual output is almost entirely unregulated. So the argument for a V-chip is stronger. It is undoubtedly going to happen over there: the four big TV networks – ABC, NBC, CBS and Fox – are finalising a common system of classification for their programmes and are due to present it to Clinton at a 'TV summit' on Thursday.

© *The Independent February, 1997*

Lost innocence of the TV children

Programmes are going to the limit, say Richard Woods and Stephen McGinty

A three-year-old girl named Angelica sued her parents last week in a dispute over broccoli. Daddy wanted her to eat her greens; she objected and hired a lawyer.

'I think we can get your parents kicked out of the house and if we play our proverbial cards right I think we can get you a generous childcare annuity on top of that,' boasted the lawyer. Angelica won possession of her parents' house and all their belongings, and complete freedom from eating vegetables.

A sad, bad and barmy tale? Welcome to children's television. That scene, from a cartoon called *Rugrats*, was beamed into homes last Tuesday on BBC1 at 4.10pm just in time to put ideas into children's heads before supper.

True, the story turned out to be a nightmare of Angelica's father. But for many parents the tone and content of children's television would disturb their sleep for real if they knew what their children were watching.

Many parents have no idea what is broadcast in the afternoon and early evening. They are, as a report from the Office of National Statistics last week made clear, too busy working longer and longer hours to know and assume safe programmes still rule the airwaves.

Get real, as Angelica might say. Children's television has kissed innocence goodbye. Kissing, indeed, is one of its favourite subjects.

After *Rugrats* it was straight into the charms of *Round the Twist* (4.35pm BBC1), an Australian drama involving a boy aged about 14. He was dreaming of locking lips with a girl in a miniskirt astride a motorbike, and found a magic potion that rendered him irresistible.

When he turned up at his girlfriend's house, her mother opened the door and promptly snogged the youngster on the doorstep. At school, girls in his class could not resist kissing him. Nor could his teacher.

Children who found this unsettling rather than amusing could have switched over to ITV. There at 4.45pm they would have found two teenage boys talking about 'kissing with no tongues', 'getting to first base' with girls, and 'fondling'.

Once upon a time – say 10 or 15 years ago – such material would not have been broadcast at a time when impressionable children might still be watching. But the proliferation of channels and pressure to compete has made programme makers push back the boundaries. Some see nothing wrong in doing so.

Amanda Harman, mother to Oliver, 7, Charlie, 5, and Sam, 3, in Hampshire, disagrees. Last week she monitored as many children's programmes as she could stand without putting a foot through the screen. She thought shows such as *Rugrats* undermined her relationship with her children.

'To show children, even in cartoon form, taking their parents for a ride or making them look weak is wrong. Children are like sponges, they take everything in,' she said.

Harman limits the amount of television her children watch, believing programmes after about 4.30pm are often unsuitable. Her monitoring confirmed that view. At 5.10pm last Tuesday, *Home and Away* on ITV included an eight-year-old boy finding a body under a bush. He casually called a friend to discuss the corpse.

Harman said: 'A lot of people think *Neighbours* and *Home and Away* are just part of the children's programmes. By seeing things like dead bodies, kids are losing their childhoods.'

The broadcasters' response is that they design schedules to cater for older children as the afternoon progresses into early evening. The same applies on Saturday mornings.

Kirsten O'Brien, who presents a Saturday magazine show on BBC1 alongside a cuddly toy aardvark, said: 'Our programming throughout the morning gets more mature. It starts off very young and by the time you get to 10.30am . . . we are going into teenagers.'

Just how mature some programme makers think teenagers are was

illustrated in a recent episode of *Love Bites*, a sex education series on ITV.

In discussing foreplay and how to be a better lover it showed two naked boys kissing in bed and a young girl sucking an ice cream and a boy's finger while a voice-over said 'licking and sucking any part of your love monster's body is foreplay'. This was just the ticket for Saturday lunch-time viewing, according to the producers.

But Dr Mallory Wober, an academic and former deputy head of research at the Independent Television Commission, believes the media professionals are out of step with the public. He says children's programmes contain more disturbing scenes than they used to and their effect is corrosive. 'There is more hairy material put in front of children now than there used to be, but their understanding of it has not accelerated,' he said.

'There is more hairy material put in front of children now than there used to be, but their understanding of it has not accelerated'

In Britain about 4 million children aged between 7 and 12 watch 3.5 hours of television a day, compared with 3 in France and 2.6 in Germany. In those countries, 97% of children do homework more than three days a week; in Britain only 42% do.

Other studies suggest television addicts, passively watching for hours each day, are prone to fail at school and turn to crime. Research by Sally Ward, a speech therapist, has identified television as a significant factor in delaying the development of language skills in very young children. Some programmes, such as *Teletubbies*, a new BBC series, are specifically aimed at babies as young as 18 months.

What should parents do? The answer, says the National Society for the Prevention of Cruelty to Children, which is to produce guidelines on coping with television, is not to throw the box away, but to teach their children to be more discriminating.

But what parents should not do is to use a diet of junk television as a substitute baby-sitter. Otherwise their offspring may say, as Bart Simpson in the cartoon series *The Simpsons* said to his father: 'You can't blame me for watching television. It's spent more time bringing me up than you have.'

© *Times Newspapers Limited, London 1997*

Violence

Information from the British Board of Film Classification (BBFC)

Hollywood's love affair with violence has been an increasing cause for concern in the nineties, yet while violence continues to sell to both the American and international markets, the trend is unlikely to end. The Board's 1996 International Conference on Screen Violence confirmed the causes for concern, which centre on the teaching of aggressive habits, the rewarding of anti-social impulses, and the fostering of increased callousness towards victims of violence through desensitisation. We know that most teenage boys, including violent young offenders, show a strong preference for action heroes, macho muscle men and former karate champions able to take on all comers. Three of the biggest action superstars, Arnold Schwarzenegger, Jean Claude Van Damme, and Steven Seagal, have excelled at making callousness macho. All three made particularly violent films in the years in question,

and each was cut by the BBFC, particularly on video where their lethal techniques could have been studied and copied by teenagers.

Since Schwarzenegger became a superstar, he seems to have tempered the brutality of his early movies in a bid for mass-market appeal, acting with small children in *Kindergarten Cop*, being tamed and humanised by the pro-social instincts of a teenager in *Terminator 2*, and reverting to the role of husband and father in *True Lies*. *Eraser*, one of the hits of 1996 in the States, was a throwback to the unforgiving hero of old – judge, jury and executioner rolled into one. If the villains were vicious, the hero was even more so, and the film required five cuts at '18' for the cinema, including a neck-break and back-break by the hero. When the film flopped in Britain, and the distributor opted to cut for '15' on video, a further 38 cuts were made in violence by villains and hero.

In all, some 3 minutes 22 seconds was cut, with the effect that the sadistic edge was removed from most of the violence, revealing a good action thriller which proved to have far greater appeal to the British audience.

If the sadism of the uncut *Eraser* was a problem, it was as nothing to the gloating, self-satisfied cruelty of Stephen Seagal in *Under Siege II*, which required 16 cuts totalling just over 2 minutes for an '18' on video, since even an '18' could not be trusted to keep the tape out of the hands of younger teenagers who find such vicious behaviour 'cool'. Another Seagal vehicle was cut for both film and video, whilst similar cuts were made in two videos starring Jean-Claude Van Damme.

The debonair new James Bond, Pierce Brosnan, had shown in *Goldeneye* the value of keeping the violence tongue-in-cheek, and the new Bond film, *Tomorrow Never Dies*, was also tailored for the '12', with cuts in violence. Meanwhile, the original Bond, Sean Connery, was adapting his violent talents to the modern mode, throwing knives, breaking necks and spraying bullets into the feet of opposing soldiers in the action adventure *The Rock*, which was cut by 15 seconds to preserve its '15' on video. Since violent blows are brief, cuts to remove them can be brief, but their excision makes a significant difference. It would be interesting to speculate why screen heroes of the nineties have become so coldly callous. One day, perhaps, the question may be answered by social historians, but it is a trend that sits rather oddly with Britain's new culture of compassion.

Maintaining appropriate limits on the violence in family films must begin by acknowledging that there is less control of audience age in the home than in the cinema. Thus where cuts have been imposed to bring a pirate adventure like *Cutthroat Island* down to 'PG', it is sometimes necessary to impose further cuts on video. When everything else in a film is gratuitous, it is perhaps unsurprising that the violence should be gratuitous as well, in this case objectionably so.

Sometimes reclassification upwards seems a better course on video than further cutting. Two of the more interesting and intelligent films of the year, *Ransom* and *Sleepers*, had been classified '15' for the cinema despite violent scenes because they were felt to have much to offer to older teenagers. On video, where parents tend to allow younger teenagers to see '15' films, it seemed better to signal that these were both films that required more maturity, and they were therefore reclassified '18'.

Material cut to reduce violence, brutality and sadism on video during 1996 included karate kicks to the head, repeated blows to the head with a club, head butts, elbow punches, innumerable men on fire, many of them deliberately incinerated, protracted torture threats to the eye in two different films, an eye-gouging in extreme close-up, other lengthy torture scenes, the throwing of knives, stabbings, throat-cuttings, the severing of fingers and limbs, and vicious and prolonged beatings-up. Blood was an issue in many scenes, particularly in Japanese Manga cartoons which revelled in gross mutilation and blood-letting, including decapitation by a passing train. Oriental films from Hong Kong and Japan seemed to specialise in grotesque, lovingly filmed violence, as if the desecration of the human body, male or female, were a cause for celebration. Most of the video violence or horror was in low-budget exploitation films in which each vicious excess led to violent retribution, with the viewer invited to savour the details in both cases.

Violent trailers were often problematic, since they set out to package violence as a pleasurable commodity, irrespective of context, and cuts were often needed during the year to counteract this.

© BBFC Annual Report
1996-97

Your guide to classification certificates

Classification certificates are given to video titles and video and computer games which are required by law to be classified pursuant to the Video Recordings Act 1984

Universal

Particularly suitable for young children

Universal

Suitable for all

Parental Guidance

General viewing, but some scenes may be unsuitable for young children

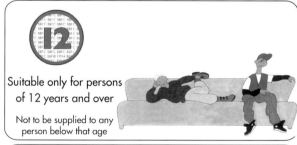

Suitable only for persons of 12 years and over

Not to be supplied to any person below that age

Suitable only for persons of 15 years and over

Not to be supplied to any person below that age

Suitable only for persons of 18 years and over

Not to be supplied to any person below that age

TV and violence

Information from the National Viewers' and Listeners' Association

Even if you watch just a few hours of TV a day, you can't miss the fact that violence is everywhere: terrestrial broadcast TV, cable or satellite. From Hollywood movies through soaps like *EastEnders* and *Brookside*, adult dramas like *Cracker* and even children's programmes like *Power Rangers*, realistic violence is the stuff of our leisure viewing.

Contrary to expectations of an improvement, the latest research report from National VALA, *More cruelty and violence 3* published in March 1997, shows TV violence worsening. Despite the horrific real life mowing down of most of a class of primary school children at Dunblane and the growing demands for stricter gun control that followed, shooting remains the commonest form of violence on screen. Our analysis of a total of 246 films on the four terrestrial channels – BBC1, BBC2, ITV and Channel 4 – in 1996 detailed a massive 1,076 incidents involving firearms, 706 violent assaults and 376 incidents involving knives or other offensive weapons. 108 films were repeat screenings – already shown at least once on terrestrial TV and now allowed to be seen once again.

These findings are a shocking disgrace. The broadcasting authorities have done little to reduce screen violence despite mounting public and Parliamentary concern. Showing such films at later times seems to be the only action taken.

The great – and the good – certainly know the power of television. Our politicians use the TV to influence us to vote for them and to explain and to justify their policies. Our leading charities use it to persuade us to part with our money. They recognise that TV has a huge influence.

But the most committed believers in TV are the advertisers and their agencies. None of them would spend the millions and millions of pounds they invest in TV every year if it did not raise awareness of the message they are selling.

One alarming message that TV – not the advertisers! – increasingly sells us is that violence is acceptable. TV says violence is trivial, commonplace, everyday, mundane. It's part of life, normal. Part of our modern culture. And it can even be funny, in a sickly ironic way.

TV violence also teaches something even more corrupting – that intelligence is out, brute force is in. Morality is out. The cops are stupid, the criminals are the clever ones. It's a jungle out there, it's every man, woman and child for themselves, and it's 'cool'.

The Broadcasting Act 1990 stipulates, in Section 6(1)(a), that 'broadcasters should do all that they can to secure . . . that nothing is included in . . . programmes which offends against good taste or decency, or is likely to encourage or incite to crime or lead to disorder or be offensive to public feeling'. This requirement also applies to the BBC through Clause 5(1)(d) of the 1996 Royal Charter.

This is the letter of the law. It sounds good on paper. But can it be enforced? Well-meaning senior broadcasters wishing to buck the trend and bring a climate of self-restraint and responsibility into their organisation must find the reality frustrating: neither the BBC nor the Independent Television Commission has the power to preview programmes or feature films, and stop them being shown if they fall short of requirements. This is the case even when the provocative nature of the programme is widely publicised in advance so more people watch!

We live in an era of increased crimes of violence against the person or property, from child abuse to wife (or husband) battering, violence at football games, 'road rage', 'joy riding', vandalism and the mugging

of the elderly or otherwise defenceless for a meagre handful of cash. TV is our single biggest influence. Many young people have seen many thousands of crimes depicted on TV by the time they reach 18. It is not unreasonable to assume, on the balance of probability, that this preoccupation with violence is bound to have harmful effects.

Violence on TV is glamorous and memorable. A scene lasting a few seconds – during a tiny part of the programme – may be remembered long after everything else in the story. Violence has a very contagious message and often produces an immediate effect. Children imitate what they see. They turn it into games where others get hurt. Violence brutalises, it coarsens and depresses others. Its impact is overwhelming and corrupting.

Many scientifically conducted research studies have concluded that watching TV violence can have an effect on the behaviour and attitudes of everyone from Polynesian islanders to urban school children in Western countries. In the UK the conclusions of these studies are often dismissed. Thankfully in the USA people across the political spectrum are beginning to accept their vitally important message. When will we wake up to it here?

Some TV producers, film directors and broadcasters laugh at our concerns about violence. They call any such outcry a 'kneejerk response'. But their entrenched view is similarly automatic. They say: 'It's realistic. It reflects reality. It's what the punters want. You don't have to watch it, do you? You can always turn off'.

But we don't have much choice, especially when these scenes are unexpected. We don't buy or rent our TVs to keep switching them off! You can't turn off your mind or fast forward something unpleasant that's being broadcast that very moment. Parents can't be there all the time to watch with their children during the hours devoted to children's programmes – nor should they have to.

TV, of course, is not the only problem. The UK's free market economy allows increasingly violent video games, computer games and videos to be sold or rented to impressionable young people And there is the worrying development of the growing number of youth magazines pushing the idea that violence is actually trendy.

But staying with TV, the imminent explosion of new digital television channels presents a very serious threat to the regulation of programme content as required by the Broadcasting Act and the BBC's Royal Charter. Without Parliamentary intervention, the inescapable result of this expansion will be that responsibility for maintaining proper standards of good taste and decency will pass irretrievably out of the hands of the regulatory authorities and into those of the programme makers and service providers. And on National VALA's past experience, safeguarding good taste and decency – not to mention reducing violence – are not the programme makers' top priority!

The powers that be in this country have yet to actually do very much about it but at least broadcast violence and its influence on children, in particular, is increasingly the subject of research and declarations of serious concern among our decision makers. We hope their words lead to meaningful actions soon. In the meantime we cannot turn our backs on those affected, the vulnerable.

• The above is an extract from *Television and Violence*, produced by the National Viewers' and Listeners' Association. See page 41 for address details.

Parents advised to vet TV viewing for the young

Research remains contradictory on link with violence. By Sarah Hall

The debate on the effects of screen violence on children will be reignited today with the publication of guidelines for parents on the issue by a leading children's charity.

The National Society for the Prevention of Cruelty to Children (NSPCC) has produced a booklet detailing the effect of violent or disturbing screen images on children of different ages.

It also offers practical advice on assessing the suitability of TV programmes, films and videos for children, supervising or limiting viewing, teaching critical viewing habits; and being aware of film classifications and the nine o'clock watershed.

Key suggestions include influencing children's attitudes by commenting on or condemning violence as it arises on the screen, and pointing out that such images do not necessarily represent real or acceptable behaviour. Child-minders should be aware of which programmes are permitted, and parents should check on their children's viewing when with their friends. Supervision of programmes watched is advised at all times – but is crucial for the under-fives, who cannot distinguish between real and fictional violence.

The leaflet – 50,000 will be distributed through the NSPCC and British Telecom shops – comes three weeks after leaked Home Office research suggested a link between violence on the screen and the behaviour of young offenders.

The two-year study, based on 120 young offenders and non-offenders, was commissioned after the 1993 murder of Jamie Bulger – whose child killers were believed to have been influenced by a video nasty found in one of their homes: *Child's Play 3*.

Concern about the influence of screen violence on behaviour has been rife since Stanley Kubrick's *A Clockwork Orange*, which provoked a series of copycat rapes and beatings after its release in 1971.

But while this most recent study has found a link between videos and violent acts, the NSPCC said research remained contradictory.

'Research does not prove one way or the other that violent images cause children to act violently, yet these images can have a negative effect,' the charity said.

Spokeswoman Hilary Cross added: 'We believe concerned parents should err on the side of caution.'

The charity's stance was supported by the industry watchdog, the Broadcasting Standards Commission, which stressed that research was inconclusive.

The director Michael Winner backed film censorship by parents, but added: 'I am certain there is no link between violence on the screen and violent behaviour.'

The guidelines were described as disappointing by a leading expert in developmental psychology, who produced a seven-page review in 1994 calling for a recognition of the link. Elizabeth Newson, emeritus professor at Nottingham University, said: 'I find it quite disappointing that the NSPCC is still shilly-shallying around and saying there is no proven link when research proves this exists.'

Murder and screen mayhem

Child's Play 3: The film was believed to have prompted the murder of James Bulger, after it was found the father of one of his boy killers had hired the video some weeks before.

Although there was no evidence the two boys watched it, there were clear parallels: In the film, a doll dressed in child's clothes is killed on a railway line after being covered with blue paint; Jamie Bulger was found on a railway line, covered with blue paint.

Natural Born Killers: Oliver Stone's 1994 film showed 52 violent deaths. Two American teenage runaways, Sarah Edmondson and Ben Darras, admitted murdering a man in a random shooting after watching the video more than 20 times. The film was also quoted by murderers in Utah, Georgia and France.

The BBC ruled it too violent to screen – but 17 per cent of children aged 10 to 12 are estimated to have seen it, according to the Broadcasting Standards Council.

Silent Witness: BBC series starring Amanda Burton as forensic pathologist. The council upheld complaints about episodes featuring a prolonged and violent domestic assault, a murder in a shower, ritualistic carvings on corpses, sexual bondage, and a body covered in maggots.

Cracker: The council upheld complaints about the hit ITV series, over a two-part episode called Brotherly Love, in which blood was seen dripping from a ceiling onto a woman, and her bloodstained dead body was shown.

The Governor: The Independent Television Commission issued a formal warning to Yorkshire Television over three scenes from the ITV prison drama shown in March.

It criticised scenes showing the governor, Janet McTeer, threatened with rape and having her fingers cut off, a rape broadcast at about 9.45pm, and a prison officer being seen having his head smashed against a lavatory.

NSPCC advice

- Take the issue of screen violence seriously.
- Protect children from unsuitable material by following the television watershed and film classification systems.
- Check TV guides, which offer explanations for classifications, such as 'contains violent scenes'.
- Watch videos or taped programmes alone first to check for suitability.
- Ensure baby-sitters or child-minders are aware which programmes are permitted and which banned.
- Influence children's attitude by commenting on or condemning violence as it arises. Children should be taught to understand that screen images do not necessarily represent real or acceptable behaviour.

© *The Guardian*
September, 1997

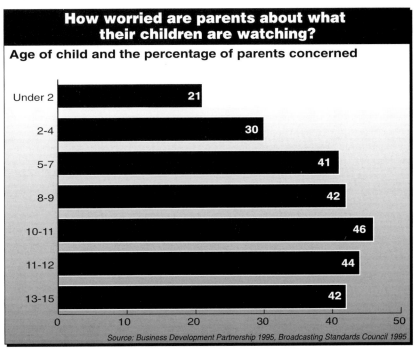

How worried are parents about what their children are watching?

Age of child and the percentage of parents concerned

Age	Percentage
Under 2	21
2-4	30
5-7	41
8-9	42
10-11	46
11-12	44
13-15	42

Source: Business Development Partnership 1995, Broadcasting Standards Council 1995

How to comment or complain

Information from the Independent Television Commission (ITC)

If you've got something to say . . .

If you want to complain, question or simply express a concern about anything on commercial television, you can do so to the Independent Television Commission (ITC). Feedback from viewers helps us to do our job effectively.

You can also contact the television company concerned directly. Commercial television companies are obliged to respond to all comments and complaints from viewers – and tell the ITC about them.

What is the ITC?

The ITC is a fully independent, public organisation set up by law under the Broadcasting Act 1990 to license and regulate all commercial television broadcast in and from the UK. We are responsible for:

- issuing licences to commercial television companies broadcasting in and from the UK. This includes the ITV companies, GMTV, Channel 4, Channel 5 and BSkyB, as well as other cable, satellite and teletext services;
- monitoring output on these services to ensure that they meet our standards;
- regulating programme content, sponsorship, advertising, teletext services and technical matters including subtitling through our codes of practice, which are available to the public.
- We do not regulate BBC1, BBC2 or S4C (the Welsh fourth channel) and some foreign services available on cable and satellite such as Eurosport, TV5 and RTL.

Regulating programmes

The ITC's Programme Code lays down strict guidelines covering:

Independent Television Commission

- taste and decency, including strong language and sexual portrayal
- violence
- privacy
- impartiality
- charitable appeals
- religious programmes
- undue prominence for commercial products

Regulating advertising

Services which we regulate have to ensure that the advertisements which they carry comply with the ITC Code of Advertising Standards and Practice and Rules on Advertising Breaks.

- Advertisements must be legal, decent, honest and truthful.
- The frequency and duration of commercial breaks are restricted. Advertisements also have to be clearly separated from programmes.

Regulating sponsorship

The ITC Code of Programme Sponsorship lays down guidelines on:

- which programmes can and can't be sponsored – and by whom;
- the content and scheduling of sponsor credits;
- commercial influence on the content of programmes.

Regulating technical standards

The ITC's engineering division in Winchester is responsible for making sure that ITV, Channel 4 and Channel 5 maintain standards of technical quality and reliability as measured against our Technical Performance Code. If you would like to raise any technical points, please contact ITC Engineering at the address given on page 41.

What the ITC can do

If you have a concern about anything that has been on commercial television, we can investigate the matter, raising it with the relevant television company if appropriate.

We may require changes that will prevent a repetition. This is particularly important in relation to advertising.

Or, for a more serious or persistent breach of the Codes, we can:

- issue a formal warning to the company.

In the most serious cases we can:

- require the company to broadcast an apology or correction;
- impose a fine;
- shorten the term of a licence or, in extreme cases, withdraw it altogether.

How to make your point

Whether you take your case directly to the television company concerned, or to the ITC, please make sure you have all these relevant facts at hand:

- the name of the television service and the programme which you were watching. Was it an ITV station, Channel 4, Channel 5, teletext, or a cable or satellite channel?
- the date and time of the broadcast, or the teletext page number;
- the exact nature of your complaint, comment or enquiry;
- in the case of an advertisement, the name of the product advertised.

You can make your point to the ITC either by telephone or in writing.

What we can't do

Before contacting us, it's worth checking whether we are in a position to help you:

- We don't make programmes or schedule them – but we are interested in whether programmes are shown at appropriate times.
- We don't preview. We can only consider programmes or advertisements once they've been broadcast.
- We can't require particular types of programmes to be shown or determine the prices charged by cable and satellite companies.
- We don't deal with transmission breakdowns. If you suspect there's a problem, call the television company direct.
- We don't consider the artistic merit or entertainment value of TV advertising.
- We cannot act simply because you do not like something in an advertisement. It has to cause offence, or have the potential to

cause harm (especially to children), or be misleading.

- We don't become involved in disputes between viewers and advertisers unless directly related to the content of an advertisement.

How do we handle your complaint?

All viewers' complaints are taken seriously and acknowledged in writing. We will investigate the complaint and send a full reply, if possible within two weeks of receiving the complaint and usually by four weeks.

Occasionally a complaint may take longer to investigate. In this case we will write to you to advise you of the reason for the delay.

We may be unable to investigate a complaint which is received long after a programme has been broadcast, as television companies are only required to keep copies of programmes for a limited period of time.

All complaints which we uphold are reported in our *Programme Complaints and Interventions Report* and *Television Advertising Complaints Report* which are published monthly and are available from any ITC office.

Every year, the ITC also reviews the overall performance of ITV, Channel 4 and Teletext (it will do the same for Channel 5). Your feedback plays an important part in compiling this report and maintaining the standard of these services which have legal obligations relating to their quality and diversity.

© Independent Television Commission (ITC)

This kind of violence isn't up our Street say viewers

It was the blow that gave TV watchdogs almost as big a headache as Curly Watts.

They are being bombarded with complaints about *Coronation Street's* violent content, with viewers particularly turned off by the soap's 'neighbours from hell', the Battersby family.

Following another big post-bag earlier this year, the Independent Television Commission last month received 79 complaints about 'taste and decency' and 'violence' in the ITV soap.

Some cited as an example the 'unwelcome change in tone in the serial and the violent behaviour of Les Battersby in head-butting his neighbour Curly Watts'.

The watchdog's report said: 'They felt this was unacceptable during family viewing time. The ITC

appreciates some viewers do not wish to see the kind of rude and dishonest behaviour exhibited by the Battersbys.'

But while acknowledging some viewers would not welcome the direction the soap has taken, the ITC did not uphold any of the complaints under the programme code.

It considered the Battersbys' behaviour was held in contempt by most Street residents, and the assault was not seen in close-up or any injury shown at the time. An ITC spokesman said: 'The issues do not breach the programme code and it is a question for TV companies whether they believe their viewers are enjoying the programme.'

The ITC received 25 complaints about a euthanasia story line in the Channel 4 soap *Brookside* concerning the decline from cancer of Mick

Johnson's mother-in-law Gladys. Most claimed the portrayal of her medical care was inaccurate, although five felt the drama wrongly promoted euthanasia. The ITC decided the portrayal was 'responsibly handled' and dismissed the complaints.

Five viewers complained about an *Emmerdale* story line in which Zak Dingle prepared to belt his son Butch with a belt over his obsession with the Tates' nanny Sophie. The ITC did not believe the scene would encourage viewers to practise this form of discipline. But it was concerned by the use of a knife in a confrontation between Sophie and Butch – not mentioned in any complaint – and informed Yorkshire Television it was at 'the margins of acceptability' for 7pm.

© The Daily Mail September, 1997

Opinion divided over effect of video violence

By Philip Johnston, Home Affairs Editor

The impact of violent videos on criminal behaviour and aggression in young people was under debate again last night.

A Home Office-backed study failed to establish a link but suggested that violent films could reinforce anti-social attitudes.

While the video industry said the report contained no evidence of cause and effect between videos and crime, campaigners for tougher controls said it was 'another crucial piece in the jigsaw'.

The research was commissioned after the murder of two-year-old James Bulger in 1993 when it was claimed that his two killers aged 10 had been influenced by watching films. While this was never proved, two psychologists at Birmingham University were asked to conduct a study.

Their report suggests that a violent home life is more likely to lead a child into crime than an appetite for videos. But it also found that violent films reinforced the anti-social attitudes of offenders already prone to violence.

They tended to identify more with 'macho' heroes, remembered the plots of violent films for longer than non-offenders and developed a taste for video violence. 'This, in turn, may reinforce distorted perceptions about appropriate means of resolving conflict and responding to frustration and provocation,' said the report.

'Offenders were more likely to prefer actors who typically play characters whose use of severe violence appears positive and successful – a dangerous role model for young people, particularly to those predisposed to crime and delinquency.'

Laurie Hall, secretary-general of the Video Standards Council, said the report showed that 'video was a side-show' compared with the effect of parental violence.

He added: 'This report provides no grounds for further restricting an industry which is already the most tightly regulated entertainment medium in Britain.'

But Jonathan Bartley, general secretary of the Movement for Christian Democracy, argued that the research strongly suggested that violent videos locked abused young offenders into a cycle of violence.

'It reveals important new evidence that violent films may indeed reinforce violent behaviour,' he said. 'This is therefore another crucial piece in the jigsaw, in giving us the full picture about the links between screen violence and violent behaviour.'

Roger Gale, Tory MP for Thanet North, said there remained a strong case for tighter controls on screen violence.

The British Board of Film Classification, which categorises videos for home viewing, has already announced a review of the guidelines used for judging their suitability and their impact on children.

Film censors maintain it is for parents and traders to ensure that unsuitable videos are not watched

by youngsters. In a statement, the BBFC said the report showed most young people were not strongly affected by video violence.

'The role of screen violence is to reinforce pre-existing tendencies,' it said.

'Unlike ordinary teenagers, violent offenders seek out violent films and videos to reinforce and validate their own violent impulses.'

The researchers monitored the viewing habits of a group of offenders and compared their reaction with young men of the same age at college. They found that exposure to violence at home and already developed delinquency tendencies were matched by an unhealthy taste for on-screen violence.

Only 11 per cent of non-offenders chose violent films as their favourite, but the figure was 25 per cent for non-violent offenders, and 64 per cent among violent offenders.

Offenders also spent significantly longer watching video films and identified with 'macho' actors such as Jean-Claude Van Damme, Arnold Schwarzenegger and Sylvester Stallone.

The report concluded: 'The implication is that both a history of family violence and offending behaviour are necessary preconditions for developing a significant preference for violent film action and role models.'

One of the authors, Kevin Browne, said the study could not prove whether or not video violence caused crime: 'Nevertheless, people who come from violent families and commit violent offences are more likely to lock into violent scenes, remember violent characters, and this may well influence their behaviour.'

Children and young persons

The issue of videos and games with age-restricted classifications and under-age children and young persons is and probably will remain the single most important problem for retailers. It is an issue in respect of which retailers must remain diligent. The fact that a retailer has not had a problem so far could change tomorrow.

Almost inevitably children, particularly teenagers, will frequently want to do things that they are not supposed to do. Obtaining a video or game that should not be legally supplied to them is certainly a challenge to many of them.

If the retailer is in any doubt as to the age of the person at the counter then the age-restricted video or game should not be supplied without proof of age. Beyond this the retailer should be aware of the inventiveness of children and teenagers and the tricks that they get up to. Some of these statements may be familiar:

'Of course I'm 18, don't I look 18?'

'It's for my dad, you can ring him if you like.'

'It's for my mum, she's parked outside on a double yellow line.'

'Here's a note from my dad.'

'It's for my mum, she's just over there.'

Retailers must remain diligent and alert to all these tricks. A mistake can result in a fine, possible imprisonment and a criminal record.

Age-suitability ratings system for games

Most games are exempt from legal classification. However, upon a strictly voluntary basis games companies who are members of the European Leisure Software Publishers Association (UK) Ltd have agreed to mark the packaging of games which are exempt from legal classification with voluntary age-suitability labels.

The labels indicate the age ranges for which any particular game is suitable having regard to the content of the game. They do not relate to the degree of difficulty of a game.

The system is designed to assist parents and others in deciding whether a game is suitable for their child or any young person under their control. It should also assist retailers when dealing with customers. It does not have any legal foundation but will give retailers more information when supplying a labelled game and customers more confidence when making a purchasing decision.

There are four age-suitability ranges designating a game as suitable for children aged from 3 to 10, children and young teenagers from 11 to 14, teenagers aged 15 to 17 and those over the age of 18. The labels for each of these ranges will appear as below:

• The above is an extract from the *Retailers Guide*, produced by the Video Standards Council. See page 41 for address details.

© Video Standards Council

Age suitability ratings for video and computer games

What to look for . . .

What they mean . . .
- A green tick in a box indicates that the content of the game **is considered suitable** for viewing by the age-group shown.
- A red cross in a box indicates that the content of the game **is not considered suitable** for the age-group shown.
- The ratings refer to the content of the game and viewing suitability – **not to the degree of difficulty**.
- Four green ticks will mean that the game is suitable for viewing by persons of all ages although the game may require a high degree of skill to play

Did you know?
- The suitability ratings are voluntary for games published by members of the European Leisure Software Publishers Association (ELSPA).
- The ratings apply to games exempt from classification under UK law. They are given in accordance with the Video Standards Council code of practice.
- Certain games are required to display a **CE** marking indicating that the game is a toy with small components and is therefore, **on safety grounds**, unsuitable for children under 36 months. Some games which are not required to display this safety marking may indicate an ELSPA age-suitability rating for children of under 3 years.

Source: European Leisure Software Publishers Association (ELSPA)

A parent's guide to computer and video games

Information from European Leisure Software Publishers Association (ELSPA)

Do you think Super Mario 64 is the dish of the day at an Italian restaurant?

If you do, don't worry, you're not alone. Across the ages, children have adopted pastimes which mystify their parents and today, with parents wearing jeans and listening to rock music in the car, it's the turn of computer and video games to baffle the older generation.

Of course, the real reason games are so popular is that they're rollicking good fun, but they're also educational and beneficial for your child. So this article is designed to give you an insight into the world of games – and also to allay any fears you may have about them.

And, if you were wondering, Super Mario 64 is widely agreed to be the best game on the Nintendo 64 system.

What's so great about games?

Ask the millions who buy them. In any given week, the most popular games can outsell the best selling singles or outgross the biggest movie hits. They're simply great fun and they can help children learn in a number of ways.

Contrary to popular belief, computer games are the opposite of mindless. Many parents like the fact that, unlike TV, gaming is an active experience for children which requires concentration and mental agility. As the National Council for Education Technology has recognised, games can help players:

- Learn to think and act quickly
- Improve attention span
- Learn from experience
- Become familiar with new technology – essential in today's hi-tech world

And games machines don't just play games. More and more families are turning to educational packages which tie in to the National Curriculum and 'edutainment' titles which blur the boundaries between learning and having fun.

Can games cause epilepsy?

No, this is a myth. Following a brief furore in 1992, the National Epilepsy Society carried out a study which proved that the condition cannot be caused by playing computer games.

Instead, a small number of people who already have 'photo-sensitive epilepsy' may discover their condition during a session on the computer or games console. However, it could just as easily be revealed by watching TV or going to a disco. The numbers are so tiny that experts can safely say that games pose no greater risk to children than other daily activities. But if you're still concerned, here are some simple guidelines for adults and children:

- Play in a well-lit room
- Take breaks
- Don't play for hours
- Don't stare too closely at the screen
- Use a monitor rather than a TV – it's sharper
- Stop if you feel unwell and see the doctor.

Will my children get addicted?

Some children may play for hours during the first flush of enthusiasm for their new hobby, but this time is a valuable learning experience. And, like anything else, the interest soon fades and playing games becomes just one part of any well-balanced youngster's life. In fact, the Department of Trade and Industry says children play on average 45 minutes a day. That's the same as one and a half episodes of *EastEnders* – only much more fun.

Overall, a healthy balance of many learning and leisure activities, is best for all the family, and a proportion of this time spent playing computer games can be enriching and fulfilling.

What if I think the rating's wrong?

At ELSPA, we go to great lengths to prevent this happening. It never has yet. The ratings system was thought out carefully with the Video Standards Council which comprises various groups concerned with children and the family. If you have any concerns over a rating, write to:
The Video Standards Council
Freepost HA4401
Greenford
Middlesex, UB4 7BR

Some facts about the industry

- About four times more games are sold in December than any other month.
- Well over two million new games consoles have been sold in the UK.
- Less than one per cent of games are suitable only for over-18s.
- The games industry is 25 years old. The first game, Pong, was put into a pub in Seattle in 1972.
- The driving simulation is the most popular games genre.
- Companies which now make games include, Disney, Microsoft and the BBC.

How can I tell which games are suitable?

Even though older players buy far more software than children, the overwhelming majority of games are still perfectly suitable for all ages. For example, the UK's best selling games are football or motor racing simulations.

Yet, a small amount of 'adult' games do exist. This is why ELSPA has introduced a system of age suitability ratings. These distinctive pack labels, clearly show the ages for which the game is suitable.

While parents should always look out for these ratings, it's worth remembering that historically, less than one per cent of releases are classified 18 and over. Nearly three-quarters are universally suitable.

Parents should also note that the ratings don't reflect how difficult a game is. So although Chess would get four ticks, it's hardly recommended for toddlers (unless they're really gifted).

Will games make my children violent?

There's far more to games than fighting and shooting. There are sports, puzzles, flight simulations, cartoon-style capers, role-playing adventures and many more. In fact, one of the industry's most successful ever games was about city planning!

Obviously some children play combat adventures and re-enact them, the same way 20 years ago they re-enacted Hong Kong Phooey and 50 years ago they re-enacted Superman comics. The violence in games would look more at home in a cartoon than a horror film – and it all arises from the kind of classic stories of good versus evil which have always captivated children.

The best advice is to watch these games with your children, then make up your own mind. And don't forget to use the ratings. Anything with four ticks will not feature graphic fighting.

The ELSPA games player's charter

Commitments and guidelines from the computer and video games industry.

The members of ELSPA agree to:
- help parents make informed choices about their children's games playing
- issue an age suitability rating for each game as a guideline for parents
- help lead the fight against pornographic and illegal software
- follow the Video Standards Council Code of Practice which includes guidelines on taste and decency

We ask parents to:
- help us encourage children to follow the simple guidelines listed below
- check what your children are playing, as you would when they are watching TV
- check they are playing games with a suitable age rating – if in doubt contact the manufacturer, the shop from which it was bought or the Video Standards Council
- look out for any pirated or illegal software and report it to your local Trading Standards Office or phone the ELSPA Hotline on 0990 133 405

We ask games players to:
- play in a well-lit room
- don't play for hours on end – take everything in moderation
- play the full distance possible (the cord's length) from the screen
- stop playing immediately if you feel unwell and consult a doctor
- if possible, use a monitor rather than a TV
- do not play if you are known to suffer from photosensitive fits

Glossary
- Budget software is widely available – PC games cost as little as £4.99.
- A console is a games machine which plugs into a TV.
- Daisy is the name of Mario's girlfriend.

- Games for the Nintendo 64 are sold as cartridges. For the PC, PlayStation and Sega Saturn they come as CDs.
- ELSPA is the trade body which represents the games business.
- Edutainment is the name given to software which combines entertainment and education.
- The Game Boy is Nintendo's hugely popular hand-held games machine.
- A joypad is the name given to a controller for a games console.
- Mario is Nintendo's best-loved games character. He's a plumber!
- Multimedia is the catch-all name given to non-games leisure software like education and reference packages.
- The N64 is Nintendo's latest console with amazing 64-bit power.
- A PC plays games but can also run business and educational software.
- The average retail price of a game is £49.99 for consoles and around £29.99 for PCs.
- Sim is short for simulation. It describes any game which recreates a real life experience, hence football sim.
- PlayStation is the 32-bit console from Sony.
- Saturn is Sega's 32-bit console.
- The Video Standards Council administers the games industries age ratings scheme.

© European Leisure Software Publishers Association (ELSPA)

Classification issues

Information from the British Board of Film Classification (BBFC)

General principles

There are no written rules, only broad guidelines, partly because standards shift in line with public opinion, but mainly because it is not possible to decide in advance what is, or is not acceptable without reference to a particular context.

The Board works on five major principles in determining the category of a given work:

- Precedent – every decision is taken in the light of a previous case, thereby ensuring consistency.
- Balancing context against detail, with due weight given to the intention of the work as well as the actual images shown.
- Decisions based on some rules, and a series of questions – e.g. there are firm rules on language in junior categories, whilst violence must always be considered in context.
- Arguments made in mitigation for specific issues, if overall the work is thought to offer positive messages to a younger audience.
- The work is always considered in terms of its likely audience – who is likely to want to watch this film, and who does it speak to.

As well as the relevant legislation, the main classification issues are:

- Violence
- Weapons
- Imitable techniques
- Sex
- Sexual language
- Sexual violence
- Drugs
- Criminal activity
- Language
- Theme
- Address

Additionally decisions are made with reference to academic and public opinion research.

Violence

The Board must pay attention to the public debate and concern surrounding the issue of media violence as well as academic research from both psychological and sociological perspectives.

We have found that the public's response is contradictory: violent films are very popular, whilst the view that there is too much violence in the media is also strongly supported. Our treatment of cinematic violence must consider its potential impact on the audience. The Criminal Justice and Public Order Act (CJPOA) amendment requires the Board to pay particular attention to possible effects on potential underage viewers. We therefore consider any encouragement or glorification of violence.

Contextual arguments are balanced against details in a number of probing questions:

- What is the overall attitude of the film towards violence?
- What is the dramatic context of the violence?
- Is the violence perpetrated by the hero or villain?
- Are there consequences or rewards for the violence?

How is the violence treated?

- Is there undue emphasis on weapons?
- Is it prolonged?
- Are there lots of close-ups?
- Is it stylised e.g. slow motion, soundtrack, editing, and do these techniques accentuate the images or restrain their impact?

How much do we see of:

- Process, e.g. blows, bullet impacts, blood spurts, etc.?
- Effects, e.g. injuries, bodies, forensic details etc.?

What is the viewer's relationship to what is shown?

- Do we identify with victim or aggressor?
- Are we repelled or excited by the violence?
- What is the power relationship between victim and aggressor?
- Is there an element of torture/sadism?
- Does the amendment to the Video Recordings Act apply? (Harm to viewer or to society through viewer's behaviour?)

We must also consider complex philosophical issues, and potential effects such as desensitisation or fear, as well as the more obvious concerns about encouraging violent behaviour. The Board debates issues such as whether more 'sanitised' versions of violence are, in fact more harmful (as some American researchers imply), because they do not show sufficiently the harmful consequences of violence. Nearly always, however, it is films which encourage the viewer to take pleasure in the pain and suffering of the victim that raise the most objections.

For example the film *Eraser* was passed at '18' for cinema release. There were some minor cuts. However, on video, we know that a number of underage viewers are likely to be attracted to this film from research on the viewing habits of teenagers. The video release was therefore significantly cut, and given a '15' certificate.

Language

The Board regularly contributes to public opinion surveys on attitudes to language, and has found that this was one of the issues that continues to offend the viewing public. In a survey by the Broadcasting Standards Council, 1991, *Taste and Decency in*

Broadcasting, respondents were asked to judge the strength of swear words. The rank order of strength has been duplicated with only minor differences in our own research on this topic through the home-viewing panel in 1997. For example words such as 'fuck' were classed as strong by 87% of respondents, 'bastard' by 59%, 'shit' by 26% and 'bloody' by only 5%.

The BBFC therefore retains very strict guidelines on language that reflect public attitudes on the issues.

'U' – occasional use of 'damn', 'hell'.

'PG' – occasional use of 'shit', 'bastard', 'bloody', 'pissed', and other low level swearing, but no sexual expletives.

'12' – as above with the rare sexual expletive.

'15' – occasional/frequent use of sexual expletives acceptable if justified by context, e.g. setting, character, dramatic use. Not always acceptable if used aggressively.

'18' – aggressive/frequent use of sexual expletives.

Sex

Public attitudes towards depictions of sex and nudity have become more tolerant in recent years, as shown in the British Social Attitudes Survey, 1996, *Portraying Sex: The Limits of Tolerance*. Nevertheless we must consider issues such as the legal age of consent and the CJPOA which refers to 'human sexual activity'. We make more general assessments about the majority of those likely to watch films depicting sexual relationships. We also consider the morality and detail in the depiction. Extended simulated sex is always '18'.

- What is the context of the sex? In a relationship/casual?
- How much on-screen detail is there? Is the sexual relationship implied, impressionistic, or explicit?
- How much nudity is there?
- Is there a scene that is included merely to titillate, or is it integral to the theme/character development?
- How is the scene shot? Does it use close-up, slow motion, un-

usual camera angles, and how do these contribute to the impact of the scene?

Sexual references and jokes:
- How graphic is the description?
- How are descriptions delivered?
- Are the references oblique or explicit? Are there alternative innocent interpretations?
- Does the humour rely more heavily on sexual sight gags?

Drugs

Our policy on drugs is determined by the idea of 'potential harm'. This is another area of widespread public concern; the issue was ranked alongside violence and language as one of the three most offensive elements in film and video, in the Board's own research *Video in View* (1992).

This issue is also caught under the Criminal Justice & Public Order Amendment to the Video Recordings Act 1994.

- What is the attitude of the film as a whole towards drugs?
- Does the particular scene advocate drug use, either directly or indirectly?
- How harmful is the drug in question?
- How is the scene shot? Does it glamorise the drug with lots of close-ups, e.g. of preparation?
- Does it instruct in how to use drugs?
- Does it focus on the ritual aspects of drug taking?

The film *Trainspotting* was passed uncut for film release, but on video some of the process of heroin preparation was cut, given the potential for the scene to be seen out of context, or by underage viewers. *Pulp Fiction* was also passed uncut on film, but a close-up of needle penetration was reframed on video, since such images have been found to be seductive for a small minority of viewers, who may be attracted to drug use.

Areas for possible cuts

Cuts are likely to be requested to the following:
- Imitable techniques – violent and criminal
  - Neck breaks

  - Double ear-claps
  - Rabbit punches
  - Hot-wiring and levering open of car doors
  - Lock picking

- Glamorisation of offensive weapons
  - Through close-ups
  - Through introduction of unfamiliar weapons

- Sexual Violence
  - Glamorised rape or sexual assault

- Material that contravenes any relevant legislation
  - Sexual explicitness that falls foul of the obscenity legislation
  - Ill-treatment of animals
  - Child protection
  - The process of violence and sadism
  - Instruction in drug use
  - Blasphemous images or dialogue

Questions

1. What are your views on the media violence debate?
2. Sex and violence are often linked in the debate on standards. Do you think this is helpful or not?
3. Given the prevalence of drugs in society, what do you think would be a responsible classification policy on this issue?
4. In many European countries, e.g. Holland, language is not a primary concern in the classification process. Why do you think the British public is so worried by this issue? What is the nature of the concern about language? Would you agree with it or not?
5. What assumptions do these classification issues make about the relationship between the audience and film or video material, and about the role of classification/ censorship?
6. Which of these issues do you think is most important and why?
7. Are there any issues missing from this that you would consider important in determining the suitability of a particular film/video?

© British Board of Film Classification (BBFC)

A parent's guide to video classification

Mum, can I watch a video? It's a very simple question and one this information is designed to help you answer.

Rules of thumb

When your child asks to watch a video there are three things you need to ask yourself:

- How old is your child?
- What do they want to watch?
- Is it suitable?

The last question is the most important. In the end it is your responsibility to make sure that your child doesn't watch anything unsuitable. And who knows your child better than you do?

Even when you do decide what your child should watch it's very difficult to control what they see, often without your knowing. It's an easy enough mistake to leave a video you may have seen by the TV when you go out, but you wouldn't leave an open bottle of whisky, packet of cigarettes or bottle of aspirins within easy reach of a seven-year-old. Think about it. Children love to do what they're not supposed to, so don't make it easy for them. Don't leave videos out which are unsuitable for your child.

Older brothers and sisters can also be a problem. There are videos which are perfectly suitable for them to see, but not when their five-year-old sister or brother is in the room.

And what are your children watching at their friends' houses? Sometimes they'll tell you and sometimes they don't. If they don't then perhaps you should find out. The fact that some parents are irresponsible doesn't mean that you should be.

Remember, in the end it's your decision.

The classifications

By law almost all videos have to be classified. The British Board of Film Classification (BBFC) is the government-appointed body designated to fulfil this task. It is a serious criminal offence to supply a video which should have been classified and which has not been.

The exceptions to the rule are videos which are educational or are chiefly concerned with sport, religion or music. You'll often see an unofficial 'E' symbol on their sleeves although the law does not require exempt titles to be marked as such.

Even one of these videos can lose this exemption. Then, by law, it has to be classified. Video titles will be classified in one or other of the following six general categories.

It's important to note that videos classified PG, U and Uc can be legally supplied to people of all ages – including children. The 12, 15 and 18 classifications restrict supply to people of the specified age and above. It is a serious criminal offence for a shopkeeper to supply a video with an age-restricted classification to someone below the specified age.

Video classifications allow you to make an informed choice for your child's video viewing. Videos classified 12, 15 and 18 are unsuitable for children or young teenagers below the specified ages. You may disagree with a classification but, if you do, then the responsibility is yours.

What do the classifications really mean?

The legal wording accompanying each classification symbol doesn't fully explain the reasons why a certificate is given. These more general descriptions may be of help:

Uc This means that the film or programme has a universal category and is suitable for everyone but especially suitable for very young children. It has probably been made just for them.

U This stands for Universal and means that the film or programme can be seen by people of all ages. There will be nothing unsuitable for children and the whole family might well enjoy it.

PG This stands for Parental Guidance which means that parents might wish to check upon the film or programme before showing it to their younger children. If it's an action film it might have some violence. If it's romantic it might have some sexy scenes or very brief nudity. It might also have some of the milder swearwords.

12 This means that the film or programme is unsuitable for anyone younger than 12. There may be stronger moments of violence or references to teenage experiences but nothing gratuitous. There may also be swearwords that you wouldn't hear in a PG video.

15 This means that the film or programme is unsuitable for anyone younger than 15. There may be a fairly adult theme or scenes of sex, violence or drugs which, while not being particularly graphic, are unsuitable for younger teenagers. There may also be some sexual swearwords.

18 This means that the film or programme is unsuitable for anyone younger than 18. There will certainly be an adult theme and there may also be strong scenes of sex or violence, which could be quite graphic. There may also be very explicit language which will frequently mean sexual swearwords.

More help

When you pick up a video you often want more information to enable you to make that final viewing decision. Although the sleeves and certificates give some indication of what the video is likely to contain, it is always helpful to have more specific information about each particular title. For example, a 15 could have some sex, violence or bad language. But does it? And if so, how much? As a result of a video industry voluntary initiative, you will have seen additional advice panels and these will be printed on even more video sleeves so you can come to your own decision about the levels of sex, violence and bad language in a title before you take it home. Short explanatory trailers have also been appearing on many releases as a final reminder of the classification before the programme begins.

After all, we have become accustomed to checking the content of the food we buy by looking at the packet, so why should videos be any different? The additional information for each title is given by the BBFC at the time that each title is being classified and is designed to help you make a more informed choice. In 1997 more video releases will carry this panel on the packaging.

A final word

The UK video industry is proud of the standards that it maintains.

It is the most restricted video industry in the free world and is subject to more legal and voluntary controls than broadcast television, cable or satellite in this country.

The issue of age-restricted videos (12, 15 and 18) and their availability to children below the specified ages will always be a major priority for the industry. A great deal has been done to ensure that unsuitable titles are not supplied to them. And this effort will continue.

However, once a video title goes through the front door parental responsibility must play its part. This article is designed to help parents make the right decisions.

There are many thousands of videos available which provide entertainment, pleasure and enjoyment to many millions of people, but some are only suitable for a more mature audience. Make sure you get it right.

Remember, in the end it's up to you.

Children like violence, so long as it is only fiction

By Alison Boshoff, Media Correspondent

Many children watch and enjoy notoriously violent 18-certificate films – but confess to feeling frightened about real life crime after watching the news.

Research on young people and the media, released yesterday by the Broadcasting Standards Council, finds that children as young as 10 seek out 18-certificate videos and like to watch violent post-watershed dramas on TV.

But although they reject censorship and say they do not feel tempted to copy violent behaviour, many confess to feeling frightened by the violence which they think surrounds them.

Sixty-six per cent of 16-year-olds said they had watched *Pulp Fiction*, the Tarantino film starring Uma Thurman, which features explicit violence and drug-taking, and a third of those surveyed had seen three or more 18-rated films.

In the 10-12 age group 17 per cent said they had watched Oliver Stone's *Natural Born Killers*, 34 per cent had watched *The Silence of The Lambs* and 23 per cent had seen *Pulp Fiction*.

An overwhelming majority of 15 and 16-year-olds – 81 per cent – said that children of their age did not need protecting, and 80 per cent said that the people who decided on film ratings did not listen to their views.

Mark Ratcliff, of the Murmur research company, which held discussion groups for the BSC, said: 'A film like *Pulp Fiction* is a laugh for the average 13-year-old. Violence in *EastEnders* can be scarier than in a Tarantino film.

'We had some 12 to 13-year-old girls who saw a TV programme called *Backup* in which a man was thrown off a block of flats.

'Instead of being disturbed by the scene some complained that the blood wasn't the right colour. Most 15-year-olds would laugh at you if you said *Pulp Fiction* was disturbing.'

But he said teenagers were sensitive to realistic violence in TV soaps or real life violence shown on the news.

In the survey, many of the respondents said they feared violence. A 13-year-old girl from Manchester said: 'The country seems so violent, all that stuff like the Wests, what happened at Dunblane, the drug wars around here. You can't go anywhere without being careful.'

Few children thought more 'real life' violence should be screened, with only 23 per cent saying the news should show a person being killed. Perhaps surprisingly, 87 per cent believed that there should be some censorship of TV to protect children younger than them from unsuitable programmes.

Watching television after the watershed was very common with average bedtimes of 10.30pm. Lady Howe, BSC chairman, said: 'The extent to which violence seems to be so much a feature of everyday as well as media life for young people has to be a worry for everyone.

'I was, however, impressed by the concern that young people show for their brothers and sisters.'

New film censor pledges review of violence in videos and games

An immediate review of the guidelines for judging the suitability of films, videos and computer games and their impact upon children was ordered yesterday by the new president of the British Board of Film Classification.

Andreas Whittam Smith, founder editor of the *Independent*, was appointed to the post by Jack Straw, the Home Secretary, after a tussle with the board over who should take over.

Mr Whittam Smith, 60, succeeds the Earl of Harewood, who retired last year after 11 years in the job. Mr Straw thwarted moves by the board to appoint Lord Birkett, a former film producer and one of two vice-presidents at the BBFC, in favour of an outsider.

The announcement of a review follows a period of controversy for the BBFC – which is funded by the film industry – over its decision to give a certificate to the film *Crash* and a perceived lack of accountability and openness.

It has also failed so far to produce an annual report for 1996 – even though it has a statutory duty under the Video Recordings Act 1984 to supply one to Parliament.

Mr Straw was further annoyed by the unilateral decision in the summer to relax the guidelines for pornographic films that can be distributed through licensed sex shops under an R18 certificate.

The president and his two deputies are appointed after consultations with the Home Secretary to watch over the activities of the board. But the real power at the BBFC has long been vested in James Ferman, its director for more than 20 years.

The board has 14 examiners who classify films for cinema viewing on an advisory basis; but it also has a statutory responsibility for videos, a task it was given by Parliament in 1985. Mr Whittam Smith's arrival is seen by campaigners for less violence and pornography as an opportunity for long overdue reform of the BBFC.

Jonathan Bartley, a spokesman for the Movement for Christian Democracy, said amendments would be tabled to the Crime and Disorder Bill currently in the House of Lords to force greater openness on the board.

'This new appointment is a step in the right direction but unless it is accompanied by legislative change, there will be no more accountability than there is now,' he said.

In particular, campaigners want the same rights of appeal against a decision to classify a video as film makers currently have under law.

The only formal legal requirement on the BBFC is to produce an annual report – but it has not published one since July 1996, which covered the previous year. A BBFC spokesman said the 1996 report was due shortly. Mr Whittam Smith acknowledged the concerns of campaigners and said one of the board's main purposes was to help parents to protect children from material which might harm them.

'I want to inspire public confidence in the classification system,' he said. 'It is likely that the main problem is going to be violence rather than sexual explicitness.' He said one possible outcome of the review might be to classify videos in a different way from cinema films 'which, after all, have a gatekeeper'.

While he was open-minded about the need for legislation, he saw the role of the board as helping parents to regulate the viewing of their children.

'I shall have that objective constantly in mind,' he said. 'I am setting in hand an immediate review of the Board's policy for classifying films, videos and digital games.'

• By Philip Johnston, Home Affairs Editor

Censored – violent videos ban for young offenders

By Patricia Wynn Davies, Legal Affairs Editor

Young offenders in institutions could be barred from watching violent videos in the light of forthcoming Home Office research which is expected to suggest that screen violence increases the rate of violence of aggressive individuals.

The results of the two-year Home Office-commissioned study, to be published in October, could put pressure on the Government to tighten censorship rules for those believed to be most easily swayed by depictions of violence in videos. Ministers are already considering a clampdown on the circulation of violent videos in secure accommodation for young offenders as part of a package of improvements being examined by the task force on youth justice to make regimes more challenging and positive.

Alun Michael, the Home Office minister, said: 'We want to look at a whole range of reforms for the youth justice system and make sure they work effectively and positively. There is a need for rational and sensible action to be taken in relation to the whole system. If the findings of this research helps in that you can guarantee that we will use it.'

The report, *The Effect of Video Violence on Young Offenders*, by Dr Kevin Browne, a forensic psychologist in Birmingham University's clinical criminology department, and Amanda Pennell, compared the reactions to violent material of normal youths with those of violent and non-violent offenders convicted of a range of serious crimes. The 120 youths in the sample, aged from 15 to 21, were questioned in detail about one video immediately after screening and reinterviewed after three and nine months. A causal link between criminal behaviour and unsuitable material in videos, films, literature or on television has never been conclusively proved or disproved by research. But Dr Browne's research is thought to be the first to study actual responses to material on screen as opposed to viewing habits.

'The more you see on television or video incidents of violence, the less shocking it becomes'

Provisional conclusions were reported yesterday to indicate that while videos would not create aggression where it did not exist before, people who already have aggressive tendencies would commit violent acts more often. Mr Michael emphasised that '99 per cent of the population see portrayals of violence, including in James Bond films, and are completely unaffected', and that it was too early to judge the quality of the research.

He said: 'The more you see on television or video incidents of violence, the less shocking it becomes. One would like to know whether there are some people who are particularly vulnerable to the images they see on video. The question is whether some people are more vulnerable to portrayals and don't make the distinction between fiction and reality.'

A Home Office spokeswoman said that the British Board of Film Classification already took account of the fact that videos were seen in the home and therefore needed to be classified more restrictively than cinema films.

© *The Independent*
August, 1997

HE WAS BANNED FROM WATCHING VIOLENT VIDEOS SO HE SMASHED HIS CELL UP!

Video statistics

Information from the British Board of Film Classification (BBFC)

The figures for classification were encouraging, with 3726 video features classified in 1996 as against 3261 a year earlier, a rise of 14%. Video trailers and advertisements were also up on the previous year. By the end of 1996, a total of 37,502 video features had been classified since the Video Recordings Act came into force in August 1985, and the total had topped 40,000 by October 1997. A table of classification certificates for 1996 shows that 46.2% of features were classified in the 'U', 'Uc' or 'PG' categories, which carry no age restriction. There were more 'PG' videos than in 1995, but slightly fewer were being cut. This was largely attributable to the success of the '12', which continued to rise as a percentage of the total, with some of the stronger 'PG' videos being classified '12' rather than cut for 'PG'. The numbers at '15' and '18' were up, too, because of increased submissions, but percentages remained similar to the previous year.

There was a significant rise in the number of cuts at '18', partly due to stricter standards on violence, but primarily because of the growing volume of sex videos, many of them British and more graphic than those submitted in previous years. Because of the risks of underage viewing under the statutory guidelines introduced in 1994, the Board had determined in 1995 that the limits of explicitness had been reached in the '18' category, and these new, more graphic submissions would have to be classified 'R18' for licensed sex shops. Because of the continuing scarcity of such licensed premises, most companies preferred the Board to specify cuts for the '18', which represented a disproportionate and wasteful use of examining time.

The Board's increased strictness was reflected not merely in a rise in the proportion of videos cut in 1996, from 6.7% of the titles to 7.1%, but also in the fact that six videos were refused a certificate altogether in 1996, the highest figure in nine years. Three of the rejects had been refused on grounds of sexual violence.

© BBFC Annual Report
1996-97

Censors claim the public is ready for more explicit videos

By Sean Poulter

Film censors have provoked outrage by arguing for the right to legalise highly explicit sex videos.

The public is more concerned about degrading and violent sex scenes than explicit ones and the rules should be changed to reflect that, they suggest.

The claim puts the British Board of Film Classification and its controversial American director James Ferman on collision course with Home Secretary Jack Straw. It will also provide ammunition for politicians and family groups pressing for the board to be replaced.

At present, sex videos should be submitted to the board for a certificate which limits their supply to people over the age of 18. If they are judged too 'strong' for general release, a 'restricted 18' category limits them to licensed sex shops and film clubs.

The board says the current rules are tight and 'it has never felt able to classify the levels of explicitness customers were looking for'.

Heavy cuts are made in the ordinary '18' category in case the videos are seen by minors and graphic material has still to be cut from 'R18' films, it says in its annual report.

The result is that distributors are bypassing the system and selling videos on a growing black market, where uncensored films containing violence, rape and female degradation are available. 'This is the harmful end of the market, yet the courts are less and less able to control it,' the board says.

Instead, it advocates bringing many videos back into the regulatory system by granting R18 certificates with the 'simple requirement' that sex in the films must be consenting, non-violent and legal.

Although the board experimented by relaxing the rules six months ago, approving two films, *Batbabe* and *Ladies Behaving Badly*, the decision infuriated the Home Secretary, who ordered a halt and review of the new policy.

Yesterday, Liberal Democrat peer Lord Alton, a campaigner for tighter rules, complained that the censors' attitude was 'quite ridiculous'. He said: 'The same logic could be used to justify legalising petty theft, simply because it is so common.'

© The Daily Mail
January, 1998

Ratings plan for Internet sparks censorship fears

Can the Internet be tamed? An international coalition wants to introduce 'ratings' for Web sites, so that parents can choose what their children can access. Charles Arthur, Science Editor, looks at the arguments over censorship

The sprawling growth of the Internet, a place where good, bad, and repulsive sites can sit cheek by jowl, may be under threat from impatient, lawmakers the United States who, in their desire to 'protect children' from unsuitable material, may end up destroying a global information resource.

An international coalition of non-governmental organisations has been trying for months to devise a workable 'ratings' system that could be used by parents in a wide range of cultures to prevent their children from accessing unsuitable material on the global network. They met last week for two days to try to thrash out the key issues.

But while the European side of the coalition, represented by the Internet Watch Foundation based in Cambridge, reckons that it will take at least 18 months to develop a workable pairing of a ratings system and software that can interpret it, the US partners and software companies have privately said that they have, at most, nine months before the US demands mandatory ratings legislation.

'We're not all fully in agreement,' said David Kerr, the chief executive of Internet Watch. 'I said at the meeting that in order to go through the necessary consultation in the various countries, you couldn't achieve it in less than 18 months. But the US side is under a lot of pressure to get it developed as soon as possible.'

The ratings would be a two-sided system, in which every site that wanted to would voluntarily compare itself against a set list of criteria, on a scale of 1 to 5, for elements such as the amount of sex, violence, nudity and strong language on the site.

Other elements, including 'intolerance – for racial items and 'dangerous activities' including cigarettes and alcohol but also sports and suicide methods, might also be offered.

The site's owner would rate the site against those criteria, and then include that rating on the site. 'We want the ratings to be as free of cultural judgement as possible,' said Mr Kerr.

At the child's computer, software in the browser would read the ratings and compare it against criteria set by the parents. Alternatively some companies might develop ready-made 'profiles' for parenting to use – so that Catholic parents could feel sure their child would not see anything they found offensive.

The self-rating system though has not proved popular. Of the tens of millions of sites on the Web, 45,000 have rated themselves. In January, the figure was 30,000. In the same time, the total number of Web sites is reckoned to have doubled.

Perversely, legislation which insists that every site must be rated for its suitability could bring the rapid growth of the Net to a shuddering halt. It would discourage people from putting new sites up, and might have unpredictable cultural effects. Some sites – such as 'news' sites, which are proliferating – are effectively unratable: would a racial war in Ethiopia, or another rail crash, be judged too intolerant or violent?

In the summer, a number of US Internet news sites broke off negotiations with the US side of the coalition on exactly this point. Mr Kerr hopes that some compromise can be reached. The signs though are not promising.

Ready-made solutions are not encouraging either. While there are a number of 'filtering' software packages written by American companies, the differences even between US and British cultures means they tend to block access to sites which British schoolchildren could find useful – including many with information about drinking, cigarettes and Aids.

Mr Kerr recognises the problems, but fears that US legislators may prove implacable, 'If it doesn't happen in a reasonable period, then the hawks and doves will be back on the legislative path in Washington,' he said.

© *The Independent*
October, 1997

Press freedom groups protest Internet censorship

A dozen press freedom groups joined together this week to protest the disturbing trend in Internet censorship in many member nations of the Asia-Pacific Economic Cooperation (APEC). The letter of protest will be presented to leaders of APEC nations at the APEC leaders' summit in Vancouver, Canada, on 24 and 25 November 1997, and has been sent to the APEC Secretariat in Singapore. The letter, co-authored by the Canadian Committee to Protect Journalists (CCPJ) and the Institute for the Studies on Free Flow of Information (ISAI) in Indonesia, states alarm over efforts by many APEC nations 'to control the free flow of information and free expression on the Internet in their respective countries'.

The letter cites examples of efforts by APEC members to control or censor the Internet. For example, 'in China, all Internet users must register with police, while all traffic on the Internet is routed through government-monitored gateways where authorities block access to a number of sites on the Internet'. Indonesia announced this year that access to the Internet would be controlled, in addition to content such as 'pornography [and] things that hamper or threaten national security'. Likewise, in Singapore, the government instituted resolutions in 1996 to regulate the whole Internet industry as a broadcast medium, including ensuring Internet service providers (ISPs) and users abide by strict guidelines against 'objectionable' content, such as pornography or 'areas which may undermine public morals, political stability or religious harmony'.

In Malaysia, the main Internet line, Jaring, states that 'members shall not use the Jaring network for any activities not allowed under any law of Malaysia.' In Japan, a non-profit organisation called the Electronic Network Consortium, which includes many computer companies, recently drew up guidelines for 'inappropriate' material on the Internet.

In Australia, the letter states, the government is attempting to implement a code of conduct for ISPs for on-line content regulation as part of a government plan to develop a 'national framework that protects Australian citizens, particularly children, from offensive or illegal material online'. In the United States, according to the letter, after the courts struck down the Communications Decency Act (CDA), which would have criminalised 'indecent' speech on the Internet, the government encouraged Internet users 'to self-rate their speech and to urge industry leaders to develop and deploy the tools for blocking "inappropriate" speech'.

In the Philippines, in 1996, the National Telecommunications Commission of the Department of Transportation and Communications solicited comments from ISPs on 'barring or blocking pornographic materials on the Internet'.

In Thailand, the state-run National Electronics and Computer Technology Centre (Nectec) in 1996, called upon local ISPs to police their own sites for pornography – those who did not comply would have their licences revoked.

The letter concludes by reminding APEC members that 'the most effective means of responding to offensive content is to counter it with more content. Censoring offensive material, through the blocking of sites or other means, will not remove it from the Internet; rather, the ease of circulating information on the Internet will simply cause the material to be duplicated elsewhere on other sites.' It also points out that 'any attempt to regulate the Internet is ultimately unworkable'.

• This letter was signed by:
Canadian Committee to Protect Journalists, Canada
Institute for the Studies on Free Flow of Information, Indonesia
Committee to Protect Journalists, United States
Freedom House, United States
Freedom of Expression Institute, South Africa
Hong Kong Journalists Association, Hong Kong
Human Rights Watch
International PEN, United Kingdom
Norwegian Forum for Freedom of Expression, Norway

© HURInet

Silencing the net

The threat to freedom of expression on-line

Summary

Governments around the world, claiming they want to protect children, thwart terrorists and silence racists and hate mongers, are rushing to eradicate freedom of expression on the Internet, the international 'network of networks', touted as the Information Superhighway. It is particularly crucial now, in the early stages of vast technological change, that governments reaffirm their commitment to respect the rights of citizens to communicate freely. A G7 Ministerial Conference on the Information Society and Development to be held in South Africa from May 13-15, 1996 should be used as a platform to repudiate the international trend toward censorship and to express unequivocal support for free expression guarantees on-line.

Restrictions on Internet access and content are increasing worldwide, under all forms of government. Censorship legislation was recently enacted in the United States, the birthplace of the Bill of Rights as well as of this new communications medium and, for better or worse, a model for other nations' Internet policies. The Clinton administration claims the law will protect minors from 'indecent' material and appears unconcerned that it will reduce on-line expression between adults to what may be deemed suitable for a child. Other democratic countries are following suit. The German phone company cut off access to all the sites hosted by an American Internet service provider (ISP) in an effort to bar Germans from gaining access to neo-Nazi propaganda on one of the sites it hosted. The governments of France and Australia have also indicated they may enact legislation to control Internet content.

Authoritarian regimes are attempting to reconcile their eagerness to reap the economic benefits of Internet access with maintaining control over the flow of information inside their borders. Censorship efforts in the US and Germany lend support to those in China, Singapore and Iran, where censors target not only sexually explicit material and hate speech but also pro-democracy discussions and human rights education.

Proposals to censor the Internet – wherever they originate – violate the free speech guarantees enshrined in democratic constitutions and international law. In the attempt to enforce them, open societies will become increasingly repressive and closed societies will find new opportunity to chill political expression.

Because the Internet knows no national boundaries, on-line censorship laws, in addition to trampling on the free expression rights of a nation's own citizens, threaten to chill expression globally and to impede the development of the Global Information Infrastructure (GII) before it becomes a truly global phenomenon. Democratic countries, including the US and Germany, that are pushing for the development of the GII will lack legitimacy in criticising efforts by China to eliminate information that 'hinders public order' or by Vietnam, where

'the cultural aspect' is cited as a reason to censor connections to pro-democracy discussions abroad.

An issue closely related to censorship is that of access, which is to a large extent determined by the existing telecommunications system. According to a 1995 report by the Panos Institute, a London-based international non-profit organisation specialising in development issues,

'Access requires a telephone line. Forty-nine countries have fewer than one telephone per 1000 people, 35 of which are in Africa. India, for example, has 8 million telephone lines for 900 million people. At a global level at least 80% of the world's population still lacks the most basic telecommunications.'

Opportunities to promote access have never been greater, however. New communications technologies are providing developing countries with an unprecedented means to leapfrog antiquated communication networks.

Limits on access are imposed by governments for a variety of reasons, including economic gain and political control. Some governments, including India and Saudi Arabia, have chosen to control the liberalising effect of the Internet by denying access to entire segments of their populations, either through exorbitant charges or by confining access to select populations, such as universities. Rather than attempting to extend the Internet to a diverse group of citizens, these governments are striving to reap the economic benefits of Internet access without making it available to economically, socially, and politically disadvantaged groups, for whom it has the greatest potential for positive change. In some countries, such as Saudi Arabia, individuals who have Internet connections through foreign-owned corporations are able to elude these restrictions.

Even at this relatively early stage in the Internet's development, a wide range of restrictions on on-line communication have been put in place in at least twenty countries, including the following:

- China, which requires users and Internet Service Providers (ISPs) to register with authorities;
- Vietnam and Saudi Arabia, which permit only a single, government-controlled gateway for Internet service;
- United States, which has enacted new Internet-specific legislation that imposes more restrictive regulations on electronic expression than those currently applied to printed expression;
- India, which charges exorbitant rates for international access

through the state-owned phone company;

- Germany, which has cut off access to particular host computers or Internet sites;
- Singapore, which has chosen to regulate the Internet as if it were a broadcast medium, and requires political and religious content providers to register with the state; and
- New Zealand, which classifies computer disks as publications and has seized and restricted them accordingly.

Privacy issues are closely related to the regulation of content and access. On-line communications are particularly susceptible to unauthorised scrutiny. Encryption technology is needed to ensure that individuals and groups may communicate without fear of eavesdropping. Lack

of information privacy will inhibit on-line speech and unnecessarily limit the diversity of voices on the GII.

The Internet has the potential to be a tremendous force for development – by providing quick and inexpensive information, by encouraging discussion rather than violence, and by empowering citizens, to cite but a few examples. But this potential can be realised only if it becomes a truly global effort. Policy makers must make every effort to ensure that internationally guaranteed rights to free expression are extended to on-line communication and call for the repeal of censorship legislation. Without such commitments, individuals face the danger of seeing their rights eroded by the very technologies they are embracing.

Net porn to get X-rating

Minister plans 'cyber patrol'. By Alan Travis, Home Affairs Editor

A British rating system for UK-built Internet websites so that parents can censor unsuitable material, including pornography, is set to be introduced by the computer industry.

The system would be similar to the traditional film classification ratings but could include warning screens and measures to block access to websites containing pornography to teenagers and children.

The move towards such a British 'cyber patrol' service comes as Home Office ministers consider what further restrictions should be imposed to control access to child and hardcore pornography and other illegal material placed on the Internet by people in Britain.

The Criminal Justice Minister, Alun Michael, is to meet the industry's watchdog, the Internet Watch Foundation, shortly to hammer out details of the new curbs.

Britain is poised to go down this restrictive route despite a US Supreme Court land-mark ruling last week against any censorship of the

Internet. The judges said an attempt by President Clinton to ban indecent material violated the constitutional right to free speech for adults.

The court argued that while a child may stumble on an indecent television programme, accessing content on the Internet involved too many steps for society to be equally concerned.

The Americans will now have to fall back on so-called cyber patrol software services which enable parents to ensure that their children cannot get access to adult material on the Internet when they are not around.

But amid growing concerns over the ease of access to pornography, particularly to child pornography, Home Office ministers are determined to ensure that Britain does not become an international gateway for the distribution of illegal material around the world over the Internet.

Mr Michael has told MPs: 'We are concerned about the presence of child pornography on the Internet and relative ease of access to such

material. With the Metropolitan Police and other interested parties, we are examining ways of controlling access to such material.'

The Home Office says that since the International Watch Foundation set up a hotline last September so that users could report the presence of child pornography sites on the Internet, it has received 94 reports covering more than 1,000 separate items from around the world. Nine of the reports raised concerns about 71 items of 'child porn' placed on the Internet by people in Britain.

The foundation has estimated that there are already 1,419 sites originating in the UK which take part in the US system of voluntary self-certification. The British sites account for 7 per cent of all those on the Internet which take part in the industry rating system.

Mr Michael says that there is no similar UK rating system available but that the foundation is to report shortly on how the self-rating system suitable for British use is to be set up.

Censor sensibilities

**Should the state control what its employees can access on the Internet?
Richard Colbey reports on a test case in the US**

The opening skirmishes are about to begin in a challenge to a Virginian law that restricts academic and public employees' access to sexually explicit material on the Internet. The American Civil Liberties Union has sought a declaration that the law, which many other states are considering introducing, violates the First Amendment's guarantee of free speech.

It requires that anyone using a government-owned computer to access or download sexual material obtains official prior approval. This applies to computers at publicly funded colleges as well as those used by government employees. Academics would usually need to request permission from the college's head of administration. All such requests would be made public. It would, as the legislators intended, obviously be embarrassing for a teacher whose subject has no call for access to sexual material to appear on the register.

However, many lecturers, particularly in subjects such as literature, gender studies and art, have claimed the law makes it impossible for them to use the Internet productively. Paul Smith, professor of English and cultural studies at George Mason University in Fairfax, has been compelled by the school to remove from his Web site sexually explicit images he had posted as examples of censorship. The basis for challenging the act is that even if permission is eventually obtained, the requirement to make the request before doing research or speaking with other academics online about sexual matters violates academic freedom and thus restrains free speech.

Supporters of the law will rely heavily on a decision of an Oklahoma court in January that rejected journalism professor James Loving's challenge to a decision by the state university to prevent campus access to sexual newsgroups. The university's ruling was based on a similar law to the Virginian one. However, as Loving did not challenge the legislation itself, merely the way his college had applied it, the issues will be different. While attempts at 'cyber-censorship' are resented in the academic com-munity, there is popular support for them in many states. The Oklahoma law was passed unanimously by both the State House and Senate. The court ruled that 'the state, no less than a private owner of property, has the right to preserve the property under its control for the use to which it is lawfully dedicated'. Academics, like everyone else, remain free to use their own computers to access 'restricted' material.

Like many censorship laws, the Virginian Act produces consequences that are far from logical 'Ironically teachers will have to get written permission to receive or send words and images that they could access without restraint in any state university library,' said Kent Willis, director of the Virginia ACLU.

In contrast with the English Obscene Publications Act which talks merely of material that 'tends to deprave and corrupt', Virginian law is very precise about what is covered. Any representation of the breast 'below the top of the nipple' unless covered by 'opaque material' offends. It also differs from the English legislation in not having any exception based on scientific, literary or artistic merit.

There is no scope for a trial as dramatic as that in 1961 when Penguin, the publishers of D. H. Lawrence's *Lady Chatterley's Lover*, were able to defend the work at the Old Bailey on that basis. However the ACLU can cite many works that academics will be constrained in their use of, including *Lady Chatterley*, Dante Rossetti's *Nuptial Sleep* and Alfred Lord Tennyson's *Lucretius*.

Europe's Internet puzzle

Free speech vs. laws against spewing hate. By Elizabeth G. Olson, New York Times Service

Geneva – The World Wide Web site of a group called the Charlemagne Hammerskins opens with an image of a man in a ski mask, carrying a gun and standing by a swastika. A click on a button below labelled, in French, 'Access for subhumans' yields a picture of what appears to be a concentration camp, accompanied by the words: 'Be assured, we still have many one-way tickets for Auschwitz.'

The site – one of a number created by groups with similar names and agendas – was carried by America Online's service in France until this month, when it was closed by administrators who decided its content was offensive.

'Putting a Nazi site on-line is illegal in France,' said Michelle Gilbert, a spokeswoman for AOL, because it 'incites racial hatred'. The site reappeared on an Internet server in Canada.

The skinhead site is hardly the only one vilifying ethnic groups. One site, based on a computer in Sweden and purporting to belong to a group called Radio Islam, is devoted to questions about the reality of the Holocaust and features caricatures of evil-looking figures with black beards and exaggerated noses, wearing Stars of David.

The hatred that drips from these and other such Web sites, of course, exists independent of any technology and occurs in all media.

But for a group of conferees meeting in Geneva this month under the sponsorship of the United Nations Human Rights Center, the question was how to apply European countries' legal prohibitions against hate speech to this new medium.

Michael Schneider, head of the Electronic Commerce Forum in Bonn, which represents German Internet service providers, said there had been several cases in which the German authorities had demanded that providers eliminate sites or face prosecution. But he argued that Internet service providers cannot control content, saying, 'They are nothing more than carriers.'

Still, Debra Guzman, director of an American organisation, the Human Rights Information Network, called the Internet 'a utopia for all kinds of hate groups, from neo-Nazis to anarchists' who are 'targeting teenage males with this propaganda'.

Agha Shahi of Pakistan, chairman of the meeting, said sites that promote racism violated a treaty against discrimination. The 148 countries that signed the pact, he said, 'are under obligation to enact measures to eliminate it'.

The United States has signed the document, but has said it will not pass laws that infringe on free speech.

The conference seemed at a loss as to how to balance what one speaker called 'the two most powerful revolutions of the 20th century, those of human rights and information technology'.

The Internet 'enables the instant marketing of hate and mayhem', said Marc Knobel, a researcher in Paris who monitors Web sites for the Simon Wiesenthal Center in Los Angeles. The number of hate sites has nearly doubled to 600 in the last year, he said; he has catalogued 300.

It is often impossible to determine who is responsible for these sites, most of which are based on computer servers in the United States.

The divergent histories of the United States, with its tradition of free-speech guarantees, and of Europe, with its World War II legacy of genocide, were evident at the conference. US representatives argued that the Internet cannot be regulated; others sought ways to ban offensive sites and punish their sponsors.

Philip Reitinger, a lawyer at the US Justice Department, said that it is 'not through government censorship that equality is well served; that principle – one which accords freedom of expression the highest respect – applies with equal force to the Internet'.

© *International Herald Tribune*
November, 1997

ADDITIONAL RESOURCES

You might like to contact the following organisations for further information. Due to the increasing cost of postage, many organisations cannot respond to enquiries unless they receive a stamped, addressed envelope.

British Broadcasting Corporation (BBC)
Broadcasting House
Portland Place
London, W1A 1AA
Tel: 0171 580 4468
Fax: 0171 637 1630
The BBC (British Broadcasting Corporation) is a public service broadcaster, operating under a Royal Charter, receiving most of its funding from the television licence fee. The unique relationship between the BBC and its audiences places on it a special obligation to serve everyone's needs and interests, and recognise the diversity of communities and cultures across the country. Services provided are BBC-1, BBC-2, and regional services, and on radio: five national networks, Radio 1, Radio 2, Radio 3, Radio 4, and Radio 5 Live; regional services; and 39 local radio stations.

British Board of Film Classification (BBFC)
3 Soho Square
London, W1V 5DE
Tel: 0171 439 7961
Fax: 0171 287 0141
The official body responsible for ensuring that all publicly shown films and videos conform to certain standards. They produce a variety of information.

British Video Association
167 Great Portland Street
London, W1N 5FD
Tel: 0171 436 0041
Fax: 0171 436 0043
The trade body representing publishers of home entertainment. Produces the leaflet *Mum, Can I watch a Video?*

Broadcasting Standards Commission
7 The Sanctuary
London, SW1P 3JS
Tel: 0171 233 0544
Fax: 0171 233 0397
The Broadcasting Standards Commission is a statutory organisation under the 1990 Broadcasting Act. Its role is to monitor the portrayal of violence, of sexual conduct and matters of taste and decency (such as bad language) in all television, radio, cable and satellite services.

European Leisure Software Publishers Association (ELSPA)
Station Road
Offenham
Evesham, WR11 5LW
Tel: 01386 830642
Fax: 01386 833871

Independent Television Commission (ITC)
33 Foley Street
London, W1P 7LB
Tel: 0171 255 3000
Fax: 0171 306 7800
Under its powers derived from the Broadcasting Act 1996, the Independent Television Commission, established under the Broadcasting Act 1990, licences commercial television services in the UK except for BBC services and S4C, whether delivered terrestrially or by cable and satellite, public teletext and certain other text and data services.

Maranatha Community
102 Irlam Street
Flixton
Manchester, M41 6JT
Tel: 0161 748 4858
Fax: 0161 747 7379
The Maranatha Community is a Christian movement which involves members of many different strands within the Christian faith.

NSPCC
National Centre
42 Curtain Road
London, EC2A 3NH
Tel: 0171 825 2500
Works to prevent child abuse and neglect in all its forms. Produces many publications on various different issues relating to children including *Screen Violence*.

National Viewers' and Listeners' Association (NVALA)
All Saints House
High Street
Colchester, CO1 1UG
Tel: 01206 561155
Works to secure effective legislation to control obscenity and pornography in the media.

INDEX

advertising, television 12, 19, 22, 232
age
    and attitude to television violence 5
    of children, and television violence 2-3
    film classification by 14, 18
    suitability for games 25, 26-7
    video classification by 25, 30-1
aggressive behaviour
    and television violence 11-12
    and violent videos 21, 24, 33
Australia, and the Internet 36

bad language
    BBFC classification of 28-9
    on television 13, 15
        public attitudes to 8, 9, 12
BBC (British Broadcasting Corporation) 7
    and sex on television 13
    'taste and decency' clause 15, 19
    and television violence 10, 21
British Board of Film Classification (BBFC) 3, 6, 7, 9, 14, 17-18
    areas for possible cuts 29
    classification issues 28-9
    and explicit sex videos 34
    review of guidelines 32
    video classifications 30, 31, 33
    and video violence 24, 32
Broadcasting Act 1990 19, 20
Broadcasting Standards Commission 8-9, 21
Broadcasting Standards Council 7, 12, 15, 21, 31

child pornography, sites on the Internet 38
children
    and age-restricted videos 25, 30-1
    latest time allowed to watch TV 15
    number of hours watching TV 14, 17
    and 'real life' violence 31
    television programmes for 16-17
    and television violence 1-3, 4, 11, 14, 20-1, 31
        and the V-chip 11, 14-15
        views on 2
    video and computer games 25, 26-7
    and violent films 31
classification
    and the BBFC 28-9
    of videos 3, 14, 30-1, 34
complaints, and the ITC 22-3
computer games
    age-suitability 25
    parents' guide to 26-7
    review of violence in 32
criminal behaviour
    and television violence 10, 19-20, 21
    and violent videos 21, 24, 33

drugs, and BBFC classification 29

ELSPA (European Leisure Software Publishers Association) 26-7
epilepsy, and computer games 26

films
    classification of 18
    review of violence in 32
    sex in 6
    on television 7, 10-11, 13
        satellite channels 9, 13
    violence in 17-18

Home Office
    and the British Board of Film Classification (BBFC) 3
    and the Internet 38
    research on video violence 24, 33

Independent Television Commission (ITC) 5, 10, 13, 14, 19
    and television violence 21
Internet 15, 35-40
    censorship 37-40
    child pornography sites 38
    Nazi sites 40
    news sites 35
    and press freedom groups 36
    ratings plan 35
    restrictions on access 37-8
        US public employees 39

nudity on television 6, 9

Obscene Publications Act 6, 7

parents
    and children's bedtimes 4
    and children's television viewing 8, 11, 16, 20-1
    guide to computer and video games 26-7
    and television violence 1-3
        views on 1-2, 8, 12
    and video classification 30-1
politicians, and violence on television 10
pornography
    and the Internet 38
    sex on television as 6
public attitudes
    research and monitoring 8-9
    to violence on television 5, 8, 9, 12

satellite channels
    bad language on 9
    'double watershed' policy 9
    films on 9, 13
sex
    BBFC classification of 29, 34
    explicit videos 34
    on television 6-7, 8, 13
    public attitudes to 9, 12, 29

television 1-27
  advertising 12, 19, 22
  bad language on 8, 9, 12, 15
  censorship and the V-chip 11, 14-15
  research and monitoring public attitudes 8-9
  satellite channels 9, 13
  violence on 1-3, 5, 8, 10-13
    and aggressive behaviour 11-12
    and children 1-3, 4, 11, 14-15, 20-1, 31
    public attitudes to 5, 8, 9, 12
  watershed policy 2, 4, 8-9, 10, 14, 21, 31

V-chip 11, 14-15
video games
  age-suitability for 25
  parents' guide to 26-7
Video Recordings Act (1984) 32, 34
videos 7
  age-restricted 25

classification of 3, 14, 30-1, 34
review of violence in 32
violent, young offenders barred from 33
and violent behaviour 21, 24
violence
  and BBFC classification 28, 29
  definitions of 5
  and pop music 13
  on television 5, 10-21
    and aggressive behaviour 11-12
    and children 1-3, 4, 11, 14-15, 20-1, 31
    public attitudes to 5, 8, 9, 12
  videos and violent behaviour 21, 24

watershed policy 2, 4, 8-9, 14, 21, 311
  satellite channels 9
women, and television violence 5

young offenders, barred from violent videos 33
young people, and video violence 24, 31

The Internet has been likened to shopping in a supermarket without aisles. The press of a button on a Web browser can bring up thousands of sites but working your way though them to find what you want can involve long and frustrating on-line searches. And unfortunately many sites contain inaccurate, misleading or heavily biased information. Our researchers have therefore undertaken an extensive analysis to bring you a selection of quality Web site addresses. If our readers feel that this new innovation in the series is useful, we plan to provide a more extensive Web site section in each new book in the *Issues* series.

*****

Books A to Z

http://www.booksatoz.com/censorship/quote.htm
Quotations on Censorship: A collection of quotes on censorship ranging from Goethe to Mark Twain. Censorship Page provides links to articles and discussions on the topic.

Censorship in Media

http://www-personal.umich.edu/~bleroy/project3/index.html
This website allows the reader to consider the issue of censorship in different media – the Internet, print, music and television. Each compartment offers background data and then presents the thoughts of prominent figures in a balanced fashion for and against media regulation. Visitors can contribute to this on-line debate.

Censorship on the Internet

http://www.ciec.org/more_background.shtml
Opposes the move to censor various sites on the internet, including personal home pages. Wants more rational policies and procedures for regulating Internet access. Electronic Privacy Information Center provides information on censorship and privacy issues on the Net. Censorship policies in India, Singapore, Indonesia and Canada are also discussed.

Feminists Against Censorship

http://www.fiawol.demon.co.uk/FAC
Feminists Against Censorship (FAC) campaigns for free expression and is opposed to all forms of censorship. Publications centre around sexual and pornographic censorship. A section is devoted to FAQs (frequently asked questions).

Index on Censorship

http://www.oneworld.org/index_oc/
Index on Censorship is a bi-monthly magazine which, through interviews, reports, banned literature and polemics, seeks to show how free speech affects the present political climate. This site provides a catalogue of abuses and restrictions of free speech and free expression around the world. Cover story confronts Hate Speech. Useful updated information on the political ramifications of censorship.

TOKARTOK: The Censorship of Art

http://www2.awa.com/artnetweb/views/tokartok/tokcen/tokcen.html
This paper addresses the censoring of artists. The author argues that the Constitutional Right to free speech takes precedent over all other liberties, including religion. Recent cases of art censorship are given.

ACKNOWLEDGEMENTS

The publisher is grateful for permission to reproduce the following material.

While every care has been taken to trace and acknowledge copyright, the publisher tenders its apology for any accidental infringement or where copyright has proved untraceable. The publisher would be pleased to come to a suitable arrangement in any such case with the rightful owner.

Chapter One: Sex and Violence on TV

What are the children watching?, © NSPCC, January 1998, *New head of film censors vows porn crackdown*, © The Guardian, December 1997, *Sex, violence, and so to bed*, © Telegraph Group Limited, London 1996, *Violence on television in Britain*, © Independent Television Commission, *Sex on TV*, © National Viewers' and Listeners' Association, *Research and Monitoring*, © Broadcasting Standards Commission, *Issues of Concern*, © Broadcasting Standards Commission, *The watershed*, © Broadcasting Standards Commission, *Does anyone really believe they'll tackle TV violence?*, © The Daily Mail, November 1996, *Violence, pornography and the media*, © The Maranatha Community, *How often do parents know what their children are watching on TV in their bedrooms?*, © Business Development Partnership, Broadcasting Standards Council, 1995, *In the US a new 'chip' will allow parents to censor TV. Could it work here?*, © The Independent, February 1996, *Number of hours of TV watched on a school day*, © Business Development Partnership, Broadcasting Standards Council, 1995, *Latest time allowed to watch TV on a school day*, © Business Development Partnership, Broadcasting Standards Council, 1995, *Lost innocence of the TV children*, © Times Newspapers Ltd, London 1997, *Violence*, © British Board of Film Classification (BBFC), *TV and violence*, © National Viewers' and Listeners' Association, *Parents advised to vet TV viewing for the young*, © The Guardian, September 1997, *How worried are parents about what their children are watching?*, © Business Development Partnership, Broadcasting Standards Council, 1995, *How to comment or complain*, © Independent Television Commission (ITC), *This kind of violence isn't up our street say viewers*, © The Daily Mail, September 1997, *Opinion divided over effect of video violence*, © Telegraph Group Limited, London 1998, *Children and young persons*, © Video Standards Council, *A parent's guide to computer and video games*, ©European Leisure Software Publishers Association (ELSPA).

Chapter Two: Classification and Censorship

Classification issues, © British Board of Film Classification (BBFC), *A parent's guide to video classification*, © British Video Association, *Children like violence, so long as it is only fiction*, © Telegraph Group Limited, London 1996, *New film censor pledges review of violence in videos and games*, © Telegraph Group Limited, London 1997, *Censored – violence videos ban for young offenders*, © The Independent, August 1997, *Video statistics*, © British Board of Film Classification (BBFC), *Censors claim the public is ready for more explicit videos*, © The Daily Mail, January 1998, *Ratings plan for Internet sparks censorship fears*, © The Independent, October 1997, *Press freedom groups protest Internet censorship*, © HURInet, *Silencing the net*, © Human Rights Watch, May 1996, *Net porn to get X-rating*, © The Guardian, June 1997, *Censor sensibilities*, © The Guardian, May 1997, *Europe's Internet puzzle*, © International Herald Tribune, November 1997.

Photographs and illustrations:

Pages 1, 4, 16, 19, 39: The Attic Publishing Co, pages 6, 10, 13, 27, 33, 35, 40: Ken Pyne.

Thank you

Darin Jewell for assisting in the editorial research for this publication.

Craig Donnellan
Cambridge
April, 1998